CHURCHES OF SOMERSET

BY THE SAME AUTHOR

Villages of England
Italian Renaissance

BRUTON. North tower *c.* 1370. West tower *c.* 1480. Clerestory *c.* 1515

Churches of

SOMERSET

A. K. WICKHAM
M.A., F.S.A.

With a Foreword by
ROBERT BIRLEY, C.M.G., M.A.
and a new Preface by
BRYAN LITTLE

DAVID & CHARLES: DAWLISH
MACDONALD: LONDON
1965

First published by Phoenix House Limited 1952
New edition published by David & Charles 1965

Printed in Great Britain by
Latimer Trend & Co. Ltd., Plymouth
and Whitstable
for David & Charles (Publishers) Ltd.
39 Strand, Dawlish, Devon

CONTENTS

To the Clergy and People of Somerset

Foreword

by ROBERT BIRLEY, C.M.G., M.A.
Head Master of Eton College

'THE ENGLISH COUNTY', we read in the Introduction to this book, 'is the most historical and usually the most convenient of local units; none more so than Somerset'—and a remarkably temperate statement it will seem to those who knew the author, with his absorbing love of Somerset and his intimate knowledge of its countryside, churches, and people. The county is, indeed, an ancient unit, older than some European countries which pride themselves on their medieval past. Of all English institutions it is the most inexplicable. No history of the organization of local government can account for it; its tenacity can only be understood by reading such a book as this, written by someone who was born in Somerset, whose forbears had lived there for many generations, and who knew it, not as a delectable land to be visited, but as his home.

A county, its life and development, can be best appreciated through its parish churches, that strange, anonymous art which unfolded itself through the centuries of its history. They, too, will only disclose their secrets to one who has known them from childhood, who has thought of them not only as artistic monuments, but as part of his own life, inseparable from his early memories and his growing awareness of the historical and the beautiful. The English nineteenth-century students of ecclesiastical architecture may have been pedantic at times and limited in their range of vision, but their work is warmed with this familiarity.

Kenneth Wickham belonged to this school of art historians, though so grandiloquent a term seems inappropriate, for they were unconcerned with theories of aesthetics and had their feet too firmly on their native soil to become lost in the cloudy realms of *Kunstgeschichte*, a word which he would only use—and it will be found in this book—with a smile. But in his study of English churches he was able to levy toll on a deep knowledge and love of the great artistic traditions of Europe, medieval and Renaissance, which enabled him to place these familiar buildings in a wider setting. And, as he himself would have held most important of all, he was the son of a much-loved Vicar of Martock and later of East Brent, two of the most beautiful Somerset churches. The parish church was to him a work of art because it was the inevitable and perfect expression of the English Church, anonymous because it represented something greater than the individual masons and craftsmen who raised the splendid towers of Somerset, the roofs in which the angels are still singing, the funeral monuments which tell of a traditional piety and trust in God.

To those who knew him, in Somerset or at Eton, it is sad that he did not live himself to see this book on which he spent so much care, but there is consolation in the fact that he was able to complete it. It is a work of scholarship, based on the writer's close personal studies of the buildings, in which full use has been made of the researches of others who have worked in the same field. But his friends will recognize throughout its pages the signs of the friendliness, the humour and the prejudices they knew so well. Those who were his pupils and the members of the Eton College Archaeological Society which he founded, will be stirred by many memories. All its readers will find themselves in the company of an individual mind and appreciate something of the devotion and charm and, not least in the many of his photographs which illustrate it, something of the patience which went to the making of this book.

R. B.

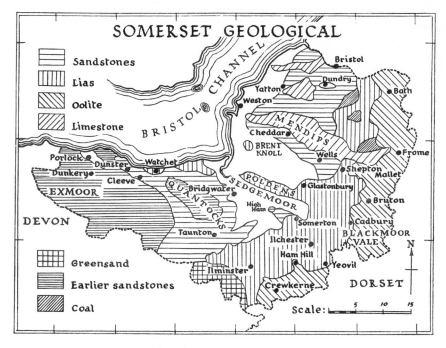

The scale is represented in miles.

Preface

by BRYAN LITTLE

IT IS BOTH pleasant and an honour to contribute a new preface to Mr. Wickham's classic work on the parish churches of Somerset. Despite the work done by locally patriotic antiquarians and county historians, few counties have yet been given adequate monographs which cover their churches not only one by one but as the well blended presentation of a firmly understood whole. Yet here, for Somerset at all events, we have a lovingly written appreciation of most of what can be displayed by a county richer than most in the architecture of its churches, and in the wealth of their fittings and monuments.

The boundaries of Somerset and those of the diocese of Bath and Wells have long almost exactly coincided. In this part of England county sentiment, and for those belonging to the Church of England, a diocesan loyalty, have roots deep in the past. Yet in the realm of church architecture and church fittings the frontiers of art and style do not always square exactly with the boundaries of local administration. For the purposes of ecclesiology West Somerset and East Devon very largely merge, while the churches of the Bristol area have much in common whether they lie in Bristol itself, in Gloucestershire, or in Somerset. Mr. Wickham was well aware of points such as these, and he did well to bring them out, though less perfectly for the interaction of Somerset and Dorset churches than for his own county's relationship with its other neighbours. But as the Ham Hill stone of South Somerset lies close to Dorset as well as to East Devon it is no surprise to find it in the medieval churches, in particular as a honey-gold adornment of towers, in the smaller county.

The main interest of this sensitive monograph must always lie in what a lifetime of observation and thinking told its author about the splendid churches of his own county. He makes it clear that apart from a few small monastic survivals like Stogursey or Stavordale his chosen subject is the *parish* churches of Somerset. Great monastic churches, like those which once stood at Bruton, Keynsham, Taunton Priory, and Montacute, have so utterly vanished that nothing need here be said of them. Wells Cathedral comes in for such items as its towers and effigies. But Bath Abbey is wholly excluded—an understandable omission in a book whose main subject is the architecture of parochial places of worship, but unfortunate when one comes to the county's otherwise unremarkable store of eighteenth-century monumental sculpture. The churches in the south of the county are apt to be more fully covered by a writer who knew more of south and central Somerset than of the Bristol end of the county with which I personally am more closely familiar.

A few paragraphs must sum up what are clearly the main historical and architectural lessons one gets from the medieval churches of this county.

Norman churches like those at Lullington and Compton Martin, the Early English chancel at Martock, and the sophisticated early Decorated work in the chancel at Ditcheat, all suggest that Somerset once had reasonable amounts of church work dating from the twelfth century to about 1350. Yet Somerset's churches are now below many other English regions in the quantity of their architecture which survives from anything but the last phase of English Gothic.

The overwhelmingly important period for Somerset churches was that which made use of the 'Perpendicular' style. For most of the main points, and in particular for a stylistic analysis of Somerset's astonishing wealth of old towers, one need do no more than study what Mr. Wickham has written. The Perpendicular style, though less exciting than the 'Decorated' which had gone before it, was capable of tremendous variety. Yet it seems, from the window tracery of some churches (and houses) built in West Somerset about the 1530's, that by then a renewed and vivid flamboyance was about to set in; one sees the point more clearly still, along with early Renaissance detail, in the panelling of the contemporary bench ends. What is also clear, from many points in Mr. Wickham's text, is that the great surge of building was even stronger in the early Tudor decades than in most of the fifteenth century. The Wars of the Roses may have deterred building more than some people have thought, and it is certainly unwise to equate 'Perpendicular' with the fifteenth century. The cloth trade was also on the increase once the Tudors had given more stable government and commercial encouragement. It was Somerset's great trade in cloth, as Mr. Wickham often points out, that lay behind the county's churchbuilding.

When the Reformation came Somerset was so well provided with churches that not many were needed in the next two centuries. Yet the county's Stuart and Georgian church architecture and furnishing is of real interest. No doubt there were once more fittings of these centuries (the superb late Georgian reredos at Martock was an example) before the *furor Gothicus* of the Victorians swept much away in favour of contents congenial to their particular taste. Somewhat surprisingly, there is little Georgian classical church architecture in Bath. Walcot church (not mentioned by Mr. Wickham) is the only Bath parish church in this style. Most of the new Anglican places of worship built in Georgian Bath were its numerous 'Proprietary Chapels', and of these only two survive, both put to secular uses. Where Bath is much richer is in its early Gothic Revival churches of the period between 1814 and about 1840. These buildings, unfortunately, were passed over by Mr. Wickham. But St. Mary's, Bathwick (by the *elder* John Pinch) and St. Michael's (by G. P. Manners) are fully worthy to stand along with the other Somerset churches of this type which are mentioned in this book.

The Industrial Revolution, and the great growth of towns in the nineteenth century, touched Somerset but lightly. Few Victorian churches were built, and in Somerset the energies of Victorian church architects mainly spent themselves in a savage bout of 'restorations'. Mr. Wickham draws attention to some of the county's

Victorian churches. He mentions and illustrates Scott's early work at Chantry, though not his church at Nailsea and his unhappy later efforts in Bath (now destroyed and replaced by a recent, much smaller building) and Taunton. But in Somerset it is to the almost wholly Victorian seaside town of Weston-super-Mare that the fanciers of Victorian churches must go. In Emmanuel the Bath architects Manners and Gill were sympathetic to the local *ethos*, while Bodley's All Saints' is worth seeing on any count.

As a county with no large modern towns Somerset does not possess many post-Victorian churches. The fair number built since 1945 are all too late for Mr. Wickham to have covered them. The outward sprawl of Bath, Taunton, and Weston-super-Mare, and Bristol's overspill into Keynsham and elsewhere, are responsible for most of those that have been put up.

Among the acknowledgements due to those who helped the author with material are those to Mr. W. A. Seaby, at that time Secretary of the Somerset Archaeological and Natural History Society, to his predecessor the late Mr. H. St. G. Gray, and to the late Mr. A. W. Vivian-Neal.

In the Somerset Archaeological Society's Library at Taunton Castle there are two most valuable pictorial records of the county's churches, made not long before the changing and destructive onset of their Victorian restorers. In the Pigott Collection are over 600 drawings of almost every old church in the county; these were made, between about 1820 and 1850, by the artist-architect John Buckler and his son John Chessell Buckler. The other collection is in the extra-illustrated copy of Collinson's *History of Somerset*. This important county history, with much of its topographical and descriptive matter by Edmund Rack, the indefatigable Secretary of the Bath and West Society, originally came out in 1791. The pictures in this amplified copy were many of them done by W. W. Wheatley for the antiquarian W. J. Braikenridge. Coming to printed books G. W. and J. H. Wade's 'Little Guide' to Somerset is a useful companion. More important, however, are the two volumes by Professor Nikolaus Pevsner which came out, after Mr. Wickham's death, in 1958. They are *North Somerset and Bristol* and *South and West Somerset* in the Penguin 'Buildings of England' series. They have their inaccuracies and omissions, but they give a most valuable conspectus by an art historian of international eminence.

Lastly, I touch on some aspects of Somerset's religious architecture passed over by Mr. Wickham. Despite the predominance of the churches used by the Anglicans any county is likely to contain some important Georgian and post-Georgian worshipping places of other religious bodies. So one cannot, in any full treatment of Somerset, disregard some of its more notable Nonconformist churches. Rook Lane Congregational Chapel, Frome, and Mary Street Unitarian Chapel at Taunton are among England's best early eighteenth-century Nonconformist churches, while at Shepton Mallet an excellent Georgian Unitarian chapel has only lately gone out of use. Such places as Beckington, Paulton, and Clutton all have pleasant chapels from soon before or soon after 1800. Bath has an excellent group of various denominations, while at Bridgwater the Baptist Chapel shows good Greek Revival work. I know little of what the Somerset Nonconformists are building now, but one at least of their Victorian buildings, the Copse Road Chapel at Clevedon, is a delicious Victorian period piece.

Among the county's Roman Catholic churches Downside Abbey is too 'cathedralesque' for this book, but others should not be disregarded. The best, perhaps, is at Shepton Mallet where the chapel and presbytery make a delightful 'churchwarden' Gothic group of 1804. Prior Park Chapel is splendidly classical by J. J. Scoles, while at Bridgwater and Yeovil are two of several Gothic churches in Somerset by one of that designer's sons who was both a priest and an architect. Bucknall's St. George's at Taunton is admirable in the Somerset late Gothic manner, and at Bath the exquisite St. Alphege's is one of the few Byzantine works by Sir Giles Gilbert Scott. Looking to the near future, a diamondwise church being built at Combe Down, and an oval one at Burnham on Sea are likely to be of exciting interest, opening out new visions of liturgical morphology.

Abbreviations used by Mr. Wickham are as follows. 'P' stands for the Proceedings of the Somerset Archaeological Society, 'S.R.S.' for the Somerset Record Society's volumes, and 'N & Q' for Somerset and Dorset Notes and Queries.

Introduction

THE LATE Dr. Allen began his work on *The Great Church Towers of England* with the proud words: 'Born and brought up in Somerset, and having a natural love of architecture, I early conceived it to be my duty to make a systematic study of the many fine towers of the county for the benefit of posterity.' The present author has the same qualifications but must claim a more modest purpose. He wishes to present the churches of his native county as a whole in a manner which shall be reliable and yet attractive. This has not hitherto been done.

The English county is the most historical and usually the most convenient of local units: none more so than Somerset, where the boundaries are natural, and have from very early times also been those of the diocese. But in most counties the churches can only be studied piecemeal or absorbed in the whole ecclesiastical architecture of England.[1] It is not of course suggested that the local style ceased at the county borders or even that the medieval builders were conscious of them, but merely that they provide to-day a casket, as it were, in which these jewels can most easily be compared and admired.

The years 1949 or 1950 are a fitting date to embark upon this task, for one hundred years ago, on the 26th September 1849, at twelve o'clock, in the Hall of Taunton Castle, the Somerset Archaeological Society held its first general meeting. It is from about that time, and greatly promoted by this Society, that the study of our churches has been critically conducted. In that study none have been more prominent or more useful than the succession of historians, antiquaries, and architects who have guided the Society in the field and then published their researches in its Proceedings. The first of these was the great Professor Freeman. His monograph, a young man's work, on *The Perpendicular in Somerset*, which appeared in 1851 and 1852 and contained a lively attack on Ruskin, can still be read with profit and has not been superseded by any comparable thesis. He says 'I have always maintained the claims of the churches of Somerset to take precedence of all specimens of parochial architecture in the kingdom. To my mind, contrary, as I am fully aware, to the general opinion, they exhibit the most perfect style of architecture in its most perfect form, and are particularly admirable for that feature, which it is well nigh the greatest boast of our English builders to have brought to perfection, their graceful and majestic towers. I generally find that the highest compliment I can pay to a church is to say that it reminds one of a Somersetshire building.' Three

[1] The admirable works of Mr. H. M. Cautley on the churches of Suffolk and Norfolk, and of Mr. R. Richards on those of Cheshire are notable exceptions.

years later, on a visit to East Anglia, he modified these opinions, but still gave the palm to Somerset for the material, the piers, the tracery and above all the towers. The superiority of East Anglia lies, as Freeman had to admit, in the larger naves, the clerestories and especially in the greater dignity of the chancels. Freeman was followed in the later seventies by Ferrey, whom we find in the eighties referred to as the Society's architect, and then by Buckle, Bligh Bond, Professor Hamilton Thompson, and since 1929 by Dr. F. C. Eeles. All these, but especially the last, have made their valuable contribution to the study of individual churches. Dr. Eeles's careful descriptions are a model of what such things should be, and the author, like every student of medieval Somerset architecture, is deeply indebted to him.

The medieval monuments and the brasses of the county have been carefully and exhaustively described and illustrated in the Proceedings of the Somerset Archaeological Society by the late Dr. A. C. Fryer and Mr. A. B. Connor respectively. Mr. Connor is carrying his lists on into the eighteenth century, but the post-medieval monuments still await their inventory. The screens, the pulpits, and the benches have been treated along with those of the rest of England by Dr. J. Charles Cox, Mr. Francis Bond, Mr. Aymer Vallance, and others, whilst Mr. Bligh Bond and Dom. Bede Camm have published two volumes on *Roodscreens and Roodlofts*. In the author's opinion there is probably room for a separate and fuller monograph on the wood-work of Somerset; some of Dr. Cox's statements in particular have been repeated unchecked for too long, but it is unlikely that future generations will find much to add to the researches of Dr. Fryer, Mr. Connor, or Dr. Woodforde, who has subjected the glass in our churches to an even closer and fuller examination. If there is another branch of local ecclesiology which needs attention, I would add that of our church bells: the work of the octogenarian Canon Ellacombe, published in 1875, is, I am informed, far from accurate and complete. There is an interesting introduction to the subject by the Rev. G. Aldridge in P 1914: H. B. Walter planned the full task in P 1920, but his full and completed manuscript lies unpublished in Taunton Castle. There are over two hundred medieval bells in our towers. The sculpture in our churches also awaits full description, and there is more of it than is commonly supposed, though in the county which contains the façade of Wells it is not really surprising. Many towers still retain some of their figures, notably Ile Abbots, and there is a wealth of minor sculpture.

It will be noted that Freeman was ahead of his time in appreciating Perpendicular architecture, which is generally regarded now as the perfect consummation of the Gothic style in this country, and one of the greatest English contributions to art. Two-thirds of the pictures which follow illustrate that style, for more than three-quarters of our four hundred ancient churches date mostly from that fine flowering time which may be said, to take a few dated examples, to begin with the building of the parish church of Yeovil in 1380 and of the south-west tower of Wells in 1386, and to be halted only by the Reformation. Rarely has the axe descended upon art so abruptly or so decisively. The Reformation had in this respect the catastrophic effect of a barbarian invasion. The long centuries before the rise of Perpendicular are sparsely represented in Somerset but the Laudian revival provided here several interesting examples, and for these opposite reasons both periods are represented generously in this book. The nineteenth century, which built some fifty new churches in the rural districts and ruined scores of others, dealt savagely with its predecessor, but a few choice Hanoverian examples, of which one (Cameley) is very little known, have survived and are here included. The author is older than Mr. Piper and Mr. Betjeman and lags behind their precocious but stimulating enthusiasms, but from a mass of the flat, the mean, and the second-rate, he has selected for his final illustrations two Victorian edifices (Chantry and Stockland Bristol) which may be a matter for wonder or interest. They, too, are a part of our *Kunstgeschichte*.

I. Romanesque

WE ENTER the church at the font, and our book may begin in the same way. The font is almost as indestructible as the waters of Baptism; someone has counted a hundred and fifty Norman fonts in Somerset; in many churches entirely rebuilt in Victorian times they are the only link with the past, and are much older than the churches then destroyed. The Victorians often, but not always, spared these venerable relics; even when they ejected or restored out of recognition so much else.

Our first example of the Romanesque font is in the extreme west, in the heart of Exmoor, at Culbone, the smallest church in England (35 feet × 12 feet) [1a]. At East Pennard and at Lullington in the east are others of the same date: at East Pennard, which is the more finished work, four sphinxes lie around the supporting column and crush four devils' heads. The font at Lullington bears the inscription *Hoc Fontis Sacro Pereunt Delicta Lavacro* and at Nempnett Thrubwell [1b] in the north the design has been rudely elaborated in the style of two centuries later.

The earliest Romanesque building in Somerset is Milborne Port, where the south wall of the choir shows Saxon pilasters, which may be of the late tenth century; the piers supporting the central tower have some capitals in stone, but some in plaster, of an unusual design of about the time of the Conquest.[1] Long and short work survives in the west walls of the aisles of Wilton in a Taunton suburb, a church which was strangely transmogrified in 1837.[2] Ashill and Thurlbear may show pre-Conquest work. At Ashill the chancel arch, although enriched later with dog-tooth moulding, retains the simple lines of eleventh-century work and is flanked by arches, now blocked, which appear originally to have been open. Remains of a similar triple arcade are visible at Thurlbear; otherwise there is little work of any importance in our churches which may be regarded as Saxon; nor, in comparison with most other districts, is there much Norman. In addition to the four churches illustrated and discussed later, we need mention only Ashill,[3] Buckland Dinham, Christon, Englishcombe, Sutton Bingham, and Thurlbear. At Buckland Dinham there are Norman door-

---

[1] *v* the late F. J. Allen and Preb. G.W. Saunders in P 1934.
[2] *v* Eeles in P 1942.
[3] A. W. Vivian-Neal in *N. & Q.*, xxiii, 29.

ways on the north and south of the nave with segmental heads. At Christon the original work is overlaid and confused by a very drastic and ambitious mid-Victorian restoration. Portions of the Norman arcades in the nave at Englishcombe have survived, and many fragments of Norman work have escaped destruction as if by mere chance. The Norman chancel arch at Sutton Bingham is of three enriched orders. Thurlbear has unusually slender nave arcades with very narrow aisles.[1] St. Joseph's chapel at Glastonbury lies outside the scope of this work. Some tower bases, arches, and doors survive in many other places, but now only appear as lonely features in later buildings. The wealth which came from the cloth trade swept away the meaner buildings of the past in order to build better ones. Antiquarian zeal and artistic vigour rarely go hand in hand: in the souls of the Reformers and the Puritans neither had any place. The Victorians, who professed a great respect for the past, thought they had the secret of its revival, and this misplaced confidence has in the end done much more damage than the ruthless but creative efforts of the fifteenth century.

An excellent example is the church of the Benedictine Priory of Stogursey, a cell of Lonlay in Normandy, sequestrated on the eve of Agincourt and granted by Henry VI to form part of the original endowment of Eton College. Stogursey lies in that strange forgotten country between the Quantocks and the sea. A cruciform church there dates from about 1100 and had apses projecting from the eastern sides of the transept. Of this church the tower, to which a spire of timber and lead was added, and the vigorous capitals of its piers survive [2a]. About 1180 the chancel level was raised and aisles were added to it. The apses disappeared and the arcades here shown were constructed [2b]. In the fifteenth century the nave levels were raised, a rood-loft erected in front of the tower, and new windows inserted throughout. Between 1829 and 1836, when Buckler made his drawing, box pews were inserted in the choir. In 1865 a reckless attempt was made to restore the Norman character of the church. The east end was rebuilt in a 'Norman style', the sanctuary raised to a great height above the rest of the choir, a ferocious 'Norman' pulpit and stone dwarf-wall were placed at its western end, deal pews and new windows appeared everywhere, and the Victorian gloom descended. No protests are recorded when the Somerset Archaeological Society visited the church in 1877, and the squire, a past President, explained to them what had been done. The redoubtable Professor E. A. Freeman, however, was not present. The enthusiasm and the actual physical labour of the present vicar have laid bare the ancient levels of the crossing, the transepts, and their apses. An altar has been placed with very happy effect under the tower, the deal pews are gradually disappearing, and, high up and far away in the east, the Victorian sanctuary is almost lost

[1] Eeles in P 1942.

to view. Unfortunately, for lack of funds and other difficulties, the work goes but slowly, and the church has been in an unwholesome state of excavation for ten years and more. A comparison between the two pictures will show how different the same building can look at different epochs [2b, 3]. A Victorian photograph, or indeed one taken to-day from a different angle, or another when the present work is completed, would show something different again.

In the east of the county near Frome are two other churches, Orchardleigh and Lullington, which the lavish care of an over-zealous squire in the fatal sixties has also wrecked—Orchardleigh irreparably. At Lullington [4] the damage is superficial but spoils enjoyment. A Victorian organ (abominably placed under the central tower), Victorian tiles, pews, and glass distract the eye from a Norman and early Gothic structure, of which the door on the north side with the corbel table above are the most striking features. The figure of Our Lord in Glory has the dignity and poise of the finest sculpture: below are heads, figures, and motifs, taken over by the Norsemen, like the centaur at Stoke-under-Ham [6a], from the mysterious symbolism of the pagan and late-classical worlds. On the capitals Samson breaks the jaws of the lion, as Our Lord broke the bonds of death, and centaurs chase a stag. Do these represent the devil or Christ in pursuit of the Christian soul? In the tympanum the Church in the guise of animals or birds feeds on the tree of life.[1] Inside the church there is the font mentioned above, and more grotesques on the pier capitals of the central tower.

The third Norman church illustrated, Stoke-under-Ham [5], is one of the most interesting and one of the most intact in the whole county; like Stogursey and Lullington, it was restored in the sixties, but in this case the restoration, conducted by Benjamin Ferrey, was tasteful and restrained. The nave and chancel are Norman, the tower (except for its battlements), the south transept, and most of the windows are of the thirteenth century. The transept, with four delicate lancets with trefoil heads on its eastern and western side, is one of the choicest things of its period. The base of the tower forms a transept on the other side. The stone, which comes from the famous hill above, is the loveliest in England. From here and from similar quarries it has shed its golden ray over almost all the churches between Taunton and Sherborne, and between the southern border and Sedgemoor. This is indeed a favoured land.

Our last Norman example is at Compton Martin which lies close under the northern escarpment of Mendip. This is an entirely different country, subject to different influences, but it may not be necessary to look as far as Durham for an explanation of the twisted column or of the early ribbed vault of the chancel. Much ingenuity has been expended to account for

---

[1] A. W. Vivian-Neal in P 1939.

the rebuilding in Perpendicular times of the Norman chancel arch and of the last bay of the nave.[1] The photograph shows a Norman clerestory which on the south side was later enclosed in a widened aisle: the fine row of corbel heads which on the north greet the visitor from the churchyard are here covered by the later roof [7]. The sockets which took the rafters of an earlier and narrower roof are exposed in the rubble walling. In 1873 Professor Freeman regretted the disappearance of a screen across the chancel, and later writers have consistently followed him, but the professor's memory is not supported by Buckler's drawing, made in 1835, which shows box pews, a high Georgian pulpit east of the twisted column, and a screen in the southern aisle, but an open chancel[2] [6b]. Above the chancel there is a room which for long was used as a pigeon house for the manor: surely a unique site.

[1] Freeman in P 1873, Bligh Bond in P 1906 and 1909, A. Hamilton Thompson in P 1936.
[2] Many mistakes would have been averted if this admirable series of drawings, made between 1820–50, of every church in the county had been known and consulted. See above, p. 12.

II. Early Gothic

THROUGH THE trefoil arch in the porch at Compton Bishop, on the south side of the Mendips, we enter into Somerset's Gothic churches, of which we have seen the beginnings at Stoke. Fine preaching crosses in the churchyards are numerous in the county, and they have often been suitably completed recently, the steps and the base alone in many cases being original [8].

The north transept of Limington, all built of Ham Hill stone, including the great slabs of the roof, which rest on a succession of closely-placed ribbed arches, is a gem of Decorated architecture [9]. Within lie the effigies, all in the same stone, of two knights and their ladies of the Gyverney family, dating from 1315 to 1330.[1] By then doubtless this transept chantry was made, for the record survives of Sir Richard Gyverney's gift of land to the church in 1329 for daily masses at the altar of the Blessed Virgin for the souls of himself, his wife, and his mother and father, to be said by John Fychet, his chaplain, and his successors for ever. It is of this church that Wolsey was later rector, of whom legend relates that he was placed in the stocks by Sir Amias Poulett for being drunk at a local fair.[2]

There are very few churches in Somerset which, like Swainswick [10], evoke at first sight the Early English or Decorated periods, the epochs so brilliantly represented in Northamptonshire and Lincolnshire.[3] The transepts and towers at Stoke-under-Ham, North Curry, Stoke St. Gregory, and Somerton; the chancels at Martock, Middlezoy, or Ile Abbots, with their eastern lancets, or at Ditcheat, South Petherton, Luccombe, Tintinhull, Bathampton, and many other places; the north aisle at Curry Rivel, the arcade and south aisle at Hemington; the nave arcades at Pilton, West Buckland, Chedzoy, or Shepton Mallet,[4] and elsewhere, are but fragments of a

[1] Fryer in P 1916–17.

[2] But see E. Chisholm-Batten in P 1886, who maintained that Wolsey at the date of his induction by proxy in 1500 was already a powerful pluralist who probably never resided at Limington and was too well protected to be thus treated.

[3] The church at Shapwick, which has a central tower but no aisles or transepts, would seem to date from about 1329. For in that year Bishop Ralph approved its erection by the Abbey of Glastonbury on a new site, the old church, whose position is still known, being too far from the village.(Somerset Record Society, ix, 27.)

[4] The interesting but depressing church of Shepton Mallet, for instance, has from the outside a Perpendicular appearance, but an examination of the piers, arches, and wall surfaces of the interior reveals the survival of the Transitional and Early English, or even perhaps of the Saxon, core. (F. J. Allen in P 1907.)

whole, and in each church except at Stoke the tracery, the tower, the roof, or the battlements sound the dominant note of the Perpendicular. For this the chief reason is the passion for church building which gripped the country after its recovery from the Black Death and which maintained its hold, fed by the wealth of the cloth trade, for nearly two hundred years. In that period the old churches were transformed and others were built new from the foundation. The central towers came down, new and splendid ones arose at the west, the naves received aisles and clerestories; larger windows and noble arcades, pews, screens, and great timber roofs appeared within, parapets, battlements, and pinnacles without. This in broad outline is the process, still in full force at the Reformation, which may be traced in the changes in style in one church after another. To understand it fully we must realize that the maintenance of the chancel was the duty of the rector, that of the rest of the church the duty of the parish. In this period the laity had more wealth available than the clergy, and delighted, from motives of devotion or personal or local pride to lavish it on their parish church. The Churchwardens' Accounts, which survive in detail from several parishes in the country, show how active was the life of the church at this time, and how money from numerous channels flowed into all its operations and raised its stones and its timbers.[1] It can therefore be seen why our chancels are so often unworthy of the rest of the church and why they, along with the chantry chapels in the transepts, more often than the nave, contain relics of earlier styles or, after a longer process of decay, have been replaced altogether by the next great revival, that of the Victorians.

With this in mind, we may look at North Curry or at Stoke St. Gregory [11], which lie on a low spur projecting into Sedgemoor and are mostly built of the local blue lias with dressings of Ham Hill. Stoke St. Gregory is the ruder and earlier structure; its tower, which is polygonal from its base, may date from the early thirteenth century, along with two windows in the south transept. The chancel is mean compared with the nave. At North Curry the transepts, tower, and nave arcades seem to have been made between 1300 and 1340. There are no capitals to the low arches of the nave and no string courses above them: the porch, the noble parapets, and, in this case, the chancel may date from the mid-fifteenth century.[2] Towards

[1] Somerset Record Society, vol. iv, Croscombe, Tintinhull, Yatton, Pilton and St. Michael's Bath, vols. xlviii, liii, lviii, and lx for Bridgwater. Volume iv has an admirable introduction by the late Bishop Hobhouse. The Bridgwater Records were the peculiar and expert province of Mr. Bruce Dilks, who faithfully transcribed and edited all the medieval documents of his adopted town; when he died in 1949, he had brought this labour of love up to Elizabethan times. See also Somerset and Dorset Notes and Queries, vols. iv, v, 1894-6, for St. John's, Glastonbury, since 1366.

[2] There is, however, some indication that the chancel was rebuilt by Peter Carslegh c. 1510. See Calendar of MSS. of the Dean and Chapter of Wells, ii, 195, 230, quoted by C. Woodforde, *Stained Glass*, p. 150.

the end of the nineteenth century it was well, but rather too expensively furnished, glazed, and repaired. There are ten other octagonal towers in the county, the most notable of which are at Somerton, of which the base may be as early as *c.* 1210, at South Petherton, and at Pitminster [12]. The latter (*c.* 1300) is at the west end and is crowned by a contemporary spire of timber and lead.[1]

All these towers are, as I have indicated, in churches where the Perpendicular, even as in North Curry, predominates. There are three or four churches where the earlier Gothic prevails. The mother church of Wells is, except for its cloister and western towers, of this earlier time, and so were at least the nave and transepts of the magnificent abbey of Glastonbury, but they lie beyond the scope of this book. The influence of the cathedral may be seen in the capitals and upper part of the piers at St. Cuthbert's Wells, which would seem to be of the early thirteenth century and were, unusually, retained when the nave was rebuilt over two hundred years later [20]. This foliage is not of the fifteenth century. We have little evidence of the architectural influence of Glastonbury in the earlier period over its vast lands in central Somerset. These stretched continuously from Mells to Weston Zoyland, with outlying villages in all directions.[2] I am inclined to think that the influence was stronger later.

Two other early churches are Witham Friary [13], wrongly so called, and Orchardleigh. The Carthusian house of Witham was founded by Henry II in the wilds of Selwood Forest in expiation for the murder of Becket. In 1176 Hugh of Avalon became its Prior, and ruled here for ten years until his appointment to the see of Lincoln. Two of the three bays of the existing church with its apse and stone vault are the work of St. Hugh, carefully preserved and restored in 1877. We must imagine here two churches, of which this is the minor one for the lay brethren, and a cloister surrounded by the cells of these monastic hermits such as may now be seen at Mount Grace in Yorkshire, or in the modern priory of Cowfold in Sussex. All but this church has now disappeared, but its severity recalls the rigorous life of the dozen monks who for two or three centuries worked with their own hands the three thousand acres of this wilderness, immune from all jurisdiction, forest, hundred, or episcopal. A strange reminder of their long loyalty to their ideal and of their eventual decline is afforded by the font, which in 1877 was found embedded in the foundations of a tower made fifty years earlier and then pulled down, when it was restored to its proper use. In 1459 a licence was obtained from the Bishop for its erection in their chapel. The monks stated in their petition that until recently all

---

[1] The others are Barrington, Barton St. David, Bishop's Hull, Doulting, Ilchester, Podymore, Weston Bampfylde.

[2] See Bishop Hobhouse's Domesday map in P 1889.

their land had been cultivated by themselves. Now in 'the decay of zeal' they had been obliged to employ lay folk of both sexes, for whom a font had become necessary. The minor church thus became parochial and since then has remained so. In Witham, then, we are in touch with the monastic establishments and with the time of their greatest glory. Glastonbury overshadows them all, but Muchelney, Cleeve, Woodspring, Stavordale, and Hinton Charterhouse are the other chief examples in Somerset. Muchelney and Cleeve have exquisite relics of the domestic buildings. Only at Woodspring and at Stavordale has anything of the church survived, and both are now incorporated in private houses.

The melancholy beauty of association alone invests the church of Witham: a different melancholy, the melancholy of Sir Gilbert Scott's restoration in 1879, surrounds the thirteenth-century church of Orchardleigh, the ancient chapel of the Champneys, which lies a few miles to the southward, on an island in a wood. Unrestored, or restored by more sympathetic hands, there could be few more beautiful things, but the romantic site, the fine array of fifteenth-century glass, and the exquisite proportions of the little building are spoilt for this generation at least by the tiles, the brown-painted drainpipes, and the harsh yellow Bath stone with which the Victorians ruthlessly renewed the quoins and the windows of the structure which they aspired to save.

III. The Great Epoch

I. ORIGINS

WITH THE building of the church of St. John the Baptist at Yeovil about the year 1380, the great epoch of Somerset architecture may be said to begin. In 1349, the year after the Black Death, an ancient feud between the rich and powerful rector and the townspeople came to a head. On a Sunday afternoon in November, while Bishop Ralph, in the course of his visitation, was attending vespers, 'certain sons of perdition, having assembled in a numerous multitude, with bows, arrows, iron bars, stones, and other kinds of arms, fiercely wounded very many of our servants of God to the abundant spilling of blood. But not content with these evil doings they entered into the said church with great strife and shut us and our servants in the said church until the darkness of the night.' Interdict on the town, and excommunication and drastic punishment of the offenders promptly followed, for in such a case the Bishop was both judge and plaintiff. Nineteen of the offenders, having confessed their crime, were ordered to hand over their arms to the vicar, to stand in a lofty place in the church during mass, bareheaded and holding a wax taper burning in their hands, and finally to go for three days through the middle of the market of Jevele (Yeovil), and there to be fustigated by a priest. The ringleader, Roger of Warmwille, was also in the same way to attend the churches and markets of Wells, Bath, Glaston, Bristol, and Somerton, to go on pilgrimage to Canterbury, and to pay £20 to the Bishop. It appears that all these punishments were duly executed.[1]

The church in which this notorious riot took place has now completely disappeared, for it was in all likelihood in expiation of this sacrilege that Robert de Samborne, the rector from 1362 to 1382 and Canon of Wells, after further successful disputes with the townspeople, began the building of a new church from the foundations.[2] His will, dated 1382, left the residue of his goods to be expended on 'the work of the church of Jevele begun by me, until it be finished'.[3] And finished it was within twenty or thirty years, and stands to-day an integral work of art, logically planned and executed

[1] S.R.S., x, p. 596.
[2] See E. Green on the Manor of Yeovil. P 1886.
[3] S.R.S., xix, p. 287.

in one style, in Freeman's words: 'One grand and harmonious whole' [14a]. Local tradition claims that it was built of stone quarried from the north side of the church where the Cattle Market now stands. Mr. Harvey thinks that the master mason was William Wynford, who designed for William of Wykeham his two colleges and the nave of Winchester Cathedral, and for Wells its western towers. The claim is based on the likeness between the arcades of Yeovil and the arches of the antechapel at New College; between its tower, especially its parapet, and those of Wells; and on the fact that Robert de Samborne was a Canon of Wells, lived there, and would have known and wished to employ one of the leading architects of his time.[1]

Twenty miles to the north-west is the ancient town of Bridgwater, and in the broad belt between Bridgwater and Yeovil the great churches lie thick. The only comparable cluster of churches in the county lies in a narrower wedge north of Mendip. It is possible to give a precise and decisive date to the church of St. Mary, which is predominantly a building of the late fourteenth century on earlier foundations and with later additions [14b]. In 1367 stone was brought down the Parrett from Ham Hill to make the spire which, until the appearance of Messrs. Courtauld's conspicuous chimney, was always the focal point of the landscape between the Quantocks and the Poldens. The spire was placed upon a tower of the preceding century, built from stone quarried in the suburb of Wembdon, where the red sandstone of the west begins. About the same time the arcades of the nave were built: enough Early English work survives on the north side to show that it was already a church of unusual size and importance. Except for numerous chantries and altars around the transepts and the east end for the service of the numerous town guilds, the fifteenth century added little to the plan of the thirteenth. Tracery of many dates is incorporated in the walls of the aisles. The Victorians added the clerestory and built the roof in a style of their own, intended to combine the wagon roof of the west with the hammerbeam of the east. There are no hammerbeam roofs in Somerset and no medieval roofs of this type anywhere. They invented another type for the chancel, where, however, they incorporated several fourteenth-century bosses.

While Yeovil is of one date and of one stone, Bridgwater covers a wider range of time and material without losing its essential unity. A large part of the exterior surface of its walls is built of the blue lias of central Somerset [14b]. In this combination of red and grey-blue and golden-grey the building before us will serve as an excellent introduction to the geological map, which is an essential aid to the appreciation of our churches. Somerset is fortunate above all other counties in the possession of three distinct types

---

[1] J. Harvey, *Gothic England*, p. 31. See the plan in P 1942, and a description by Mr. John Goodchild, sold in the church.

of building stone. The oolite belt, which from Lincoln to the Dorset coast is the geological backbone of England, enters Somerset near Bath and continues down its eastern and southern side as far as Crewkerne. It provides the yellow stone of the quarries near Bath, the grey stone of Doulting from which Wells and the churches on both sides of Mendip are built, and finally the glorious golden stone of the south. The softer and coarser lias formations fringe the oolite to the west, and from various quarries above Somerton and the Polden Hills provided a cheap and easily worked material for the moorlands and the low-lying country of the centre. At Bridgwater the red sandstones begin and cover all the county to the west. Those which fringe the Quantocks afford a beautiful stone for the solid walls and towers of local churches, but neither sandstone nor lias is easily worked: the one is too hard and the other too soft, and in both these areas fine work is either avoided or supplied from the quarries of the southern limestone, of which the most famous is Ham Hill. Hence in the immediate neighbourhood of the southern quarries we shall find whole villages built of their stone, like Martock or Montacute, and naturally the churches, too; as we move farther north we shall find the villages built of lias and the churches increasingly so. The governing factor is always the cost or the difficulty of transport, and as we have seen at Yeovil and in the tower of Bridgwater the material was, wherever possible, extremely local. Modern transport and the Industrial Revolution have unfortunately almost eliminated such considerations. In the single street of Long Load the two stones meet, mingle for a short time and then are entirely lias in Long Sutton and entirely Ham Hill in Stapleton and Martock.

Such in broad outline are the surface geological conditions, but there are big outliers of the sandstone north of Mendip, and in them again little islands of limestone like Dundry. Ubley and Stowey and Cameley are red; the tower of Clutton has bands of white alternating with a delicate pink tufa. No church or any building of note can be appreciated without recognizing the material of which it is built: even by means of the half-tone blocks of this book one may recognize the three stones of Bridgwater to which all three areas of Somerset have fitly contributed. Their colours are usually but relative, for all these stones decline towards grey, but there are times when the strong sunlight seems to draw from them an absolute value. Then Bishop's Lydeard [41] is red indeed, Somerton is blue indeed, and Norton gold indeed, or Kingston [49] is gold and red and Ile Abbots [47] and North Petherton [52] are blue and gold—the latter is the most frequent combination.

The illustrations which follow are intended to show the development of the larger Perpendicular church. Another of early date is Congresbury [15a] whose spire was erected and nave rebuilt in the fourteenth century.

Its north arcade has been thought[1] to provide the earliest known example of the pier which becomes almost universal in Somerset in the Perpendicular period, one with four little attached shafts and a separate capital to each, such as may be seen in the photographs of Dunster [63a], Martock [21], Long Sutton [24], Weston Zoyland [25], Axbridge [74b] and Muchelney [73]. The clerestory at Congresbury is altogether unusual in the west: the wealth of windows, two to each arch, recalls East Anglia [15a]. The spire, like most of the other eighteen in the county[2] is of the Decorated period. The roof is also of an early type, wagon and ceiled, with large square bosses at the intersections of the purlins and the principals. As at Banwell and in the aisles at Yatton, the timber-work is carried down from the wall plate to cover the spandrels of the clerestory, and terminates in a series of small painted figures.

With Congresbury it is natural to compare the neighbouring church of Yatton [15b] which, apart from its weak and truncated spire, is one of the noblest in the county. The stone is the grey stone of Dundry and nowhere is the masonry more accomplished. A cruciform Norman church has disappeared, but seems to underlie all later developments in plan. The lower stage of the tower with the transepts dates from about 1340. The lower lancet in the south face of the tower may be the relic of the first Gothic reconstruction one hundred years before. The nave, with its clerestory and aisles, was rebuilt about 1440: stone was being brought from Dundry for the tower and spire in 1456. On the north side the Newton chapel [68a] was built in the lifetime of Sir John Newton who died in 1487 and was buried in the stone wall-tomb within. Near him is the alabaster tomb of his father, Sir Richard, a judge, who died in 1448. From the resemblance of this chapel to the chain gate at Wells we may perhaps place its date at about 1465. Very beautiful, too, are the well-balanced west front; the south porch [29] with the fine ogee curves of its delicate panelling; and the parapets composed of trefoils within a triangle which are continued all round the church, as at Wrington [38].

We have records of the later stages of this work in the Churchwardens' Accounts which begin in 1445 and continue beyond the Reformation.[3] They throw a flood of light upon the church life of the times. At Bridgwater the funds were collected by a compulsory church rate elaborately arranged and, if necessary, enforced in the Courts Christian. The more normal procedure in the smaller places was followed at Yatton, where the sums were raised by voluntary contributions; these were collected by visit-

[1] By E. Buckle in P 1899.
[2] Bridgwater, Chiselborough, Compton Pauncefoot, Corston, Croscombe, Doulting, East Brent, Frome, Kenn, Kingston Seymour, St. Mary Redcliffe, Trent (formerly in Somerset), Ubley, West Harptree, Whatley, Wolverton, Worle, Yatton.
[3] S.R.S., iv.

ing officials called lightmen and also raised by periodical church ales, later held in the house built for the purpose, which would be the equivalents of a modern bazaar and a modern parish room. One of these church houses still exists at Crowcombe.[1] To these church ales the Newton family doubtless contributed generously but it is evident that the bulk of the money came year by year from a population of yeomen and peasants. When one remembers this and multiplies these sums by at least twenty to get the rough modern equivalent, one sees how great, and increasing to the end, was their devotion and their pride in their church. Thus we find that in 1457, £31 is paid to John Crosse, the village carpenter, for the rood-loft, which has since disappeared. Sixty-nine figures for it cost £3. 10s. 4d. In 1455 we read 'For ale gevyn to Crosse yn certeyn tymis to make hym wel wellede (well-willed) 2d.' In 1482 a suit of vestments and a cope bought at Bristol cost £26, in 1499 a processional cross £18. A new altar in honour of St. Catherine was installed in 1503, painting and gilding in 1512 cost £12. 16s. 8d., the churchyard cross was erected of the best Bath stone in 1524, new organs cost £12 in 1528, and another suit of vestments and a cope were bought for £30 in 1534.[2] All this in addition to ordinary building and repairs. In 1549 expenditure of a different sort begins, and it is much cheaper: 'Payd for takyng down our Lady in the chaunsell 4d.' or 'Thys yere the sylver crosse of owr church was sold . . . and the money bestowyd upon the makyng of a sirten skusse [sluice] agenste the rage of the salte water'. After the Marian interlude, in which the old expenses occur again, this continues in 1559: 'for takyng downe the Roode 5d., at the plucking down of the Images 6d.' By 1582 the accounts show that the spire was weakening, and in 1595 it was reduced to its present unfortunate proportions.[3]

The earlier type of church in Somerset was cruciform in plan and had an octagonal tower or a spire. The cruciform plan, but with a central tower rebuilt in Perpendicular times, survives in the important churches of Crewkerne, Wedmore, and Axbridge. At Ilminster the whole church as it exists to-day, except for some disastrous alterations to the nave in 1825, dates from the fifteenth century. The plan, but no visible part of a previous structure, was maintained. The north transept of this church, with its unusually elaborate parapet, was built to house the fine tomb with its noble brass of Sir William Wadham, who died in 1452. The tower was probably built about 1500, and the chancel by the rector, the Abbot of Muchelney, some twenty years earlier [19]. In my opinion, the transept was not completed until after the tower.

[1] P 1908.
[2] In 1508 a previous organist had been buried: 'for the pavyng of Harye Organs pytt 4d.'
[3] P 1922.

Wedmore lies very well on the last of the low ridges of the central moors, and looks towards Mendip [16b]. Underneath a rich accretion of fifteenth-century buildings, the cruciform plan of its earlier church, which survives in the base of the tower, is still apparent. The nave was never heightened to rise above the aisles, and pinnacles never appeared in the tower. A dignified parapet of pierced trefoiled panels surrounds the tower top, and the same design unpierced flows round the strange irregular outline of the walls, whose original shape is obscured by two chapels and a lofty, tower-like porch. The low vestry on the south-east which was here when Buckler did his drawing in 1831 has now gone. A photograph from the same angle is impossible [16a].

There is a similar but more regular plan at Axbridge, where again an earlier church laid the conditions for what we now see [17a]. The chancel and the transepts with their wagon roofs may be of the late fourteenth century; the rest of the building was rebuilt in the fifteenth. Thus the heavy arches of the tower were encased in Perpendicular mouldings, panels, and fan vaulting. The arcade on the north of the nave was built first, that on the south side later in the century, if we may judge from the moulded capitals on the north side and those with foliage on the south. The north arcade of the chancel whose capitals are adorned with angels will be later still.[1] A better-known view of this church is from the town square on the south side, whence a long curved flight of steps rises to the porch and the eye is carried from there to the tower above, and all is crowned with parapets of continuous quatrefoils interspersed with pinnacles. Two figures have survived in the tower, St. John the Baptist, the patron of the church, to the east, and a king, perhaps Henry VI, to the west.

At Crewkerne the only trace of the earlier church is the lowest stage of the tower. A built-up thirteenth-century window on the north side, and the relatively low massive arches of the crossing, though concealed by Perpendicular features, betray an earlier building. All else was rebuilt in Ham Hill stone in the second half of the fifteenth century [17b]. From all sides rises a rich array of battlemented parapets with heavy turrets, and a vigorous orchestra of heads and beasts and grotesques cling to their string-courses; the nave, unlike Axbridge and Wedmore, has a clerestory, and the proportions of the west front are almost as noble as those of Yatton. The western doorway and the great window above it are the finest in the county. As at Wedmore and Axbridge, there seems to have been an earlier rood to the east of the tower, and then a later one across its western arches. The last and richest part of the church is the north transept with great windows and fine panelled timber roof.[2]

Each of the four churches which we have just examined, though altered

[1] F. C. Eeles in P 1945.　　　[2] F. C. Eeles in P 1939.

greatly in the late fifteenth century or early sixteenth century, retains its central tower. Examples of those where, along with the rebuilding of the nave, the transformation was completed by the removal of the central tower and the erection of a new one to the west, are St. Cuthbert's Wells [18a] and Martock, and perhaps also Kingston [49] and St. John's, Glastonbury [18b]. At Wells there is documentary evidence of the survival of the central tower until the mid-sixteenth century, over a hundred years after the building of the great tower at the west; at Martock there is structural evidence as strong. The documentary and structural evidence at Glastonbury and Kingston, respectively, is weaker, but at least it strengthens the probability that churches of their importance would have possessed a tower before the fifteenth century and that that tower would have been central. The central towers or transepts of pre-fifteenth century date which survive are sufficient to suggest the wide dispersal of the type in the bigger churches of Somerset. More we cannot say. The evidence at Wells is a collection made by the Mayor in 1561 for 'The newe making and settynge uppe in church where the styple did stand'.

At Martock [28] and Glastonbury the projection of a transept through the south aisle can easily be seen; the transeptal plan makes a central tower likely; at Martock the argument is strengthened by the outward lean of the choir walls; arches had been pierced in these walls to give access to chapels made in the fifteenth century, and they were thus less able to support the tower.[1] At Glastonbury the Churchwardens' Accounts of about 1465[2] mention damage caused by the fall of the pinnacles of the tower: possibly this was followed by its complete removal before the building of the western tower shortly afterwards. At Kingston the nave arcades and the aisles of an Early English church remain; this was completely transformed—chancel, windows, parapets, woodwork—three hundred years later. The bench-ends provide a date, 1522, and the source, a shuttle, of all this lavish expenditure: the tower is all of that time; had there been one at the west before, part of it would surely have been incorporated in the new construction. The same argument, which admittedly falls far short of positive proof, induces the belief that many of our great Perpendicular churches with western towers conceal an earlier and quite different plan. Positive proof, other than that we have in a few cases, might be afforded when a rare and thorough restoration lays bare the foundations of a chancel or of the east end of a nave.

However, the church where an enlargement from modest origins to

[1] Preb. G.W. Saunders, Notes on Martock, *Western Gazette*, 1935, and reprinted separately.
[2] N. & Q., iv, 235; the condition of the documents renders it impossible to fix this date precisely.

the perfected type can most easily and surely be traced above ground to-day is Bruton [Frontispiece]. Apart from the absence of an original central tower, this might almost be taken as the *locus classicus* of Perpendicular development. Dr. Eeles has described the process very clearly.[1] In two hundred years the people of Bruton gradually transformed the small early structure of their ancestors into the noblest church of east Somerset. The first stage was the building of a new chancel in the early fourteenth century. This was destroyed in 1743, but its position is determined by the crypt which still survives. Towards the end of this century a north aisle and a tower were added to the nave; this tower, which was still of modest dimensions, also survives and serves as porch and chief entrance. In the early fifteenth century the nave itself was rebuilt, and a rood-loft was introduced, the remains of whose staircase can still be seen. The great west tower was then built about 1480. To bring the new nave into scale, a clerestory and new roofs were found necessary, and these were completed by 1520. The Reformation left to the eighteenth century the erection of a chancel in its turn on a scale, if not in a style, commensurate with the rest.

2. CHRONOLOGY

We are on surer ground when we pass to the main purpose of this book, which is the appreciation of what survives rather than an inquiry into what preceded it. The illustrations are intended to show the sure taste of the Perpendicular designers and the excellence of their work. Enough documentary evidence exists within the county alone to control within about fifty years the dating according to style. We have seen this evidence at Bridgwater, at Yeovil, and at Kingston. It will be sufficient to outline the rest. In the year 1423 Lady Elizabeth de Botreaux (née Daubeney of South Petherton) was granted a licence to found a college of seven secular priests in the church of North Cadbury '*per ipsam de novo edificata et constructa*'. To the fourteenth-century tower, she added then, about the year 1420, the church as it stands to-day, symmetrically constructed with a two-storied porch and otherwise identical elevations on each side; her tomb with the effigies of herself and her husband, removed from the chancel, now lies neglected under the tower [23, 26b]. There is in existence the contract made with John Marys of Stogursey for building the tower of Dunster, dated 1443.[2] The date 1482 occurs on the tower of Dundry, and 1529 on a stone shield outside an east window in the north aisle at Minehead. Two of the last abbots of Glastonbury, John Selwood (1456–93) and Richard Bere (1493–1524), put their initials on work which they promoted. Contrary to expectation these are found not only in the chancels whose upkeep was

[1] P 1933, pp. 1–18.   [2] P 1906, p. 59.

their responsibility as rectors, but also in other parts of the church, which seems to show that the monks did not always take a minimum view of their duties. Thus *J.S.* occurs on the bench-ends of East Brent and on the parapet of the chancel at Ditcheat and of the south aisle at Meare. *R.B.* may be seen on the porch at Chedzoy and on the transept at Weston Zoyland. The evidence of wills proves the rebuilding of St. Mary's at Taunton, and especially of its splendid tower, between the years 1488 and 1514;[1] the tower of West Buckland in 1509;[2] the tower of Hill Farrance in 1540;[3] the unfinished tower of Ruishton between 1530 and 1535;[4] the tower of Batcombe in 1540; and of Chewton Mendip in 1541.[5] In 1533 John Toker of Dunster left to the building of the tower of Old Cleeve 'my toker's shers [fuller's shears] that be with Barnard Dovell'.[6] Other legal evidence dates the chancel of Bishop's Hull between 1523, when there was a dispute about the contract before its erection,[7] and 1540, when it was hallowed.[8] Bishop Fox granted a licence for the consecration of Long Sutton in 1493,[9] stated then to have been entirely rebuilt [24]. A shield, marked 1513, serves to date the magnificent roof of Martock [58].

At High Ham evidence of another sort is available: an Elizabethan rector, Adrian Schaell (1570–99), 'a germane' from near Leipzig, wrote in the parish register in 1598, 'as well for the love of antiquity as for the commodity of the parish', a lengthy memoir which he describes as 'a breife compendious description . . . lest the remembrance of that church newly erected from the foundation should utterly perish'. For according to his circumstantial account[10] the church, except the tower which is of the fourteenth century, was built within one year, 1476, by John Selwood, John Dyer the parson, Sir Amias Poulett, and others. The rector, John Dyer (1459–99), as his brass in the chancel states, was responsible especially for the choir [55]. The names of many others of the laity, whose concern would have been the nave, are mentioned, and the abbot as patron seems to have subscribed to both parts of the church. Tradition, which I have been unable to verify, holds that the church of Wellow was built by Sir Thomas Hungerford, first Speaker of Parliament, in 1372. Gerard's *Particular Description of Somerset*, written in 1633, attributes to one John Heron, the portreeve of that place, the rebuilding of the church at Langport about

---

[1] P 1908, 30; S.R.S., xvi, p. 279, etc., see the index to the volume.
[2] S.R.S., xix, 137; P 1935, p. 55.
[3] N. & Q., xvii, p. 119.
[4] P 1898, p. 31.
[5] P 1915, pp. 86, 99.
[6] F. W. Weaver, *Wells Wills*, p. 77.
[7] N. & Q., vii, p. 264.
[8] N. & Q., xvii, p. 119.
[9] P 1894, p. 37. S.R.S., lii, p. 183.
[10] P 1894, p. 114.

1485. His arms are in the fine glass in the east window along with those of his friend Amias Poulett. The portcullis of Lady Margaret Beaufort, lady of the manor, appears on the battlements of the tower.[1] A popular tradition, supported by her piety, has ascribed to her the building of many of our churches, but the legend, though by no means improbable, is not upheld by much evidence. The evidence of heraldry fixes the clerestory and the roofs of the aisles and nave at Bruton between 1506 and 1522, for the mitre and dolphin of Richard FitzJames, Bishop of London between those years, and founder of the King's School, who came from Redlynch, two miles away, appears among them. Documentary evidence places the great screen of Dunster in 1499, and that of Banwell in 1521 [63b]. Dated bench-ends are at Trull (1510), Crowcombe (1534), Spaxton (1536, and 1561), North Cadbury (1538), Milverton (1540), Chedzoy (1559) (and also M and a crown for Queen Mary), Trull again 1560. The last-named, which is quite distinct from the earlier and main work of Trull, is signed by the carver Simon Warman, whose name also appears on the probably rather earlier work at Broomfield. Finally, at Broomfield and at four other churches between 1532 and 1535 we find money left for the building of new aisles. These were at Corfe (now destroyed), Exford (by the blacksmith), Hinton Blewett ('for a window in the new yeld') and Nettlecombe. The pictures of Broomfield [32] and, of Ile Abbots [33] show, inside and out, the character of this late work.[2]

It will be noted that most of these dates and all the dated woodwork are of the sixteenth century. In the building or reconstruction of a church the woodwork would have been the last thing made; indeed, pews did not become general until towards the end of the Middle Ages, and it would seem that in Somerset and East Anglia there was then a general rush to make them. At the same time pulpits and elaborate rood screens were also being lavishly provided. Even when allowance is made for the fact that, except on tombs, dates were rarely, if ever, placed on buildings or their fittings before the end of the fifteenth century, it is obvious that all this evidence indicates a great increase in the tempo of church building on the eve of the Reformation. The evidence of style supports this contention and proves abundantly that in the west country at least, far from a decline there was an actual increase in the devotion of the people to the church, in their pride in its fabrics, and their delight in its worship. Never before or since has so much money been spent on the parish churches of England as in the half-century before the last bad years of Henry VIII.

[1] Her emblem, 'Three daisies on a turf', may be seen in quarries in the Deanery at Wells, and also in the nave at Sherborne Abbey.

[2] F. W. Weaver, *Wells Wills*, pp. 82, 83, 84, 110, 162. I am grateful to Mr. J. Harvey for drawing my attention to some of these dates.

3. THE DEVELOPED STYLE

We are now at liberty to examine the quality of Somerset Perpendicular in the design and development of the bigger churches, leaving their most splendid features, the towers and the roofs, and also a few minor examples, for separate consideration.

St. John's Glastonbury [18b] and Martock [28] both show, as we have seen, traces of the transeptal plan, obscured by the erection of aisles and their windows at a later date. Glastonbury is built of the local lias faced with dressings of stone of the Doulting sort; Martock is built throughout of the stone of Ham Hill from two miles away. At Martock a chancel with an east window of five lancets survives from the thirteenth century; at Glastonbury the chancel, though built at the same time as the nave, is unworthy of it and of the great Abbey across the road which provided the funds. The townspeople were much more lavish in their share of the work. South porches projecting beyond the line of the aisles are common to both churches. The whole work at Martock—buttresses, plinth, string-courses, and parapets—is much more finished and complete. Inside there is the arcade which Freeman admired and which may indeed be regarded as the sure and logical perfection of the style [21]. Each proportion, member, and ornament fits naturally into the whole and happily supports the glorious roof. The panel work in the spandrels, the triple tiers of shield-bearing angels, the clerestory windows with a richer and later design than those of the aisles below, form a perfect composition. We may only regret that the niches were bereft of their saints by a Roundhead visit in 1645 to celebrate the taking of Bridgwater, and that the Restoration paintings are an inadequate substitute. These niches, and indeed the whole arcade, compare very favourably with a similar one at Taunton, where the canopies are too cramped and the modern statues too obtrusive.

The arcade at St. Cuthbert's Wells shows the slender and unusual effect produced by the re-use early in the fifteenth century of material made two hundred years earlier: the lower eight feet of the columns were made to match the old, and set between the old bases and the old short columns, capitals, and arches [20]. Such respect for the past, even if caused by financial rather than aesthetic or sentimental considerations, is very rare in the Middle Ages: even the famous example in the nave of Westminster Abbey is not so remarkable as this: the medieval builders, unlike many modern architects, were not also antiquarians.

A comparison of the nave at Queen Camel [22] with the three succeeding examples will show from what the Perpendicular style developed. Here the low, squat main arcade is of the Decorated period; nearly all else, windows, clerestory, roofs, screen and pulpit, come from the late fifteenth century. The church belonged to Cleeve Abbey, and the noble screen, like the chancel bosses or the stern imposing tower, may show influences from the monks or from the west. Monastic influence is also perceptible in Elizabeth de Botreaux's fine church at North Cadbury [23]. For a Somerset church the chancel is unusually large and high, and like so many, it has been ill-used by the Victorians; the windows are set high enough to allow room for the chaplains' stalls and canopies below; the arcade, which we may place at about 1420, differs in its more elaborate mouldings but not in its proportions from the ordinary Perpendicular type in Somerset.

This type, which we first found at Congresbury at the end of the fourteenth century, had become general in the county a hundred years later. It may be seen at Long Sutton [24], Weston Zoyland [25], or High Ham. The naves of these churches may be regarded as typical of the style in its final development, both in structure and fittings. At Long Sutton we have seen that the date is about 1490. At Weston Zoyland a recent restoration (c. 1935) has brought back a rood screen and a plaster surface to the walls. Long Sutton was restored much earlier, when naked interior walls were the mistaken fashion. Walls were always plastered in the Middle Ages, and normally covered with painting; over the chancel arch and above the rood we should imagine a Doom; on the north side, opposite the entrance by the south porch, the tall figure of Saint Christopher as at Ditcheat strides through the waters with the Christ Child on his shoulders; above the main arches and in all other places there are Madonnas, Crucifixes, and legends of the saints. These paintings were hidden but preserved by coats of Reformation whitewash, and where the plaster has been undisturbed they have come to light again all over England in the last twenty or thirty years. Partly owing to the drastic treatment of the walls by the Victorians very few, however, have survived in Somerset. The most notable is the thirteenth or fourteenth-century Dormition of the Virgin at Sutton Bingham, where enough survives to show the extreme beauty of the lines [26a]. In rapt devotion the Apostles stand with upraised hands and inclined heads round the prostrate form of the Mother of God. If, however, we may judge from the Christopher at Ditcheat, the St. George at Farleigh Hungerford, and examples outside the county, the paintings of the Perpendicular period were quaint and crude more often than they were beautiful.

The lovely little church of Broomfield in the Quantocks has an arcade which was doubtless built with the north aisle in 1535.[1] The wood carving on the benches, the wall plates of the roof, and the floriated capitals of the columns are typical of the west of the county and of Devonshire, where perhaps something of a Celtic imagination and love of ornament survived [32].

[1] F. W. Weaver, *Wells Wills*, p. 82.

Plates 26b and 27 show two southern elevations seen at midday. It is contended that they reveal in two or three particulars the development of the style during the fifteenth century: (1) North Cadbury (*c.* 1420) has tracery of the rather bald type which we find at the beginning of Perpendicular (*cf.* Yeovil, Axbridge, the aisles of St. Cuthbert's Wells, Wedmore west front, Yatton, or Bridgwater, all of which may reasonably be dated before 1450). (2) Norton-sub-Hamdon has the richer type, springing from ogee-headed lights, which prevails in its later stages, but also the single deep hollow moulding in the splays of the windows which we sometimes find at an earlier date (*cf.* Yatton, St. Cuthbert's Wells), but which becomes far more common, almost universal, later (*cf.* Crewkerne [17b], Martock [21], Ile Abbots [33], Ashington [72]. (3) Finally the straight and broad parapets of Cadbury have been greatly improved at Norton, where they are broken by battlements and integrated with the buttresses by pinnacles and gargoyles. If this tentative comparison has any value, it will serve to prove how favourably the style was developing and how its latest buildings were the best.

Behind the east end of Norton appears a slope of Ham Hill, whence the stone for the whole exquisite building came. Within, it is unusually lofty and beautiful, but its proportions, like those of Cannington, where too a single roof covers nave and aisles, defy photography. Close by at Cadbury is the great Tudor house built by Sir Francis Hastings long after the time of Elizabeth de Botreaux. Like those at Mells or at Brympton [35b], it may act as a reminder that at least some of our churches were built by and dependent on the great landowners, and were not, like most of those we have seen, the joint work of the parishioners. Mells was a manor of Glastonbury, and tradition has it that John Selwood had much to do with its erection. The houses of Cadbury and Brympton have changed hands frequently since the churches were built.

The porches of Mells [30] and Curry Rivel [31] show work characteristic of north and central Somerset. Leland describes the church at Mells as being built in 'time of mind' which would place it, at latest, at the end of the fifteenth century. The fan-vaulting of the ground floor both here and at Curry Rivel will confirm this date. Like other North Somerset churches, such as Doulting, Wellow, or Yatton [29], the dominant motif in the design is the big ogee curve, in this case twice repeated and especially bold and dynamic in the parapet. A different effect is obtained in the soft Ham Hill stone of Curry Rivel, behind which rises in harsh contrast the rebuilt blue lias tower. Here a charming band of quatrefoils displays on shields the Beaufort portcullis and the feathers of the Prince of Wales (Arthur's or perhaps Edward VI's), the fiddles and the bagpipes sound lustily overhead, and a little company of beasts and grotesques crouch above the aisles and on the set-offs of the buttresses. The aisle windows with their transoms and tiny quatrefoiled circles are a rare reminder to the eastward of the style of West Somerset (Selworthy, Crowcombe [35a] or Cleeve).

From here it is not far in miles or in sentiment to the north side of Ile Abbots, seen in the evening sunlight [33]. It is said, though I do not know on what evidence, to have been built by Lady Margaret Beaufort, who died, after her son, in 1509, though the depressed arches, the more elaborate parapet, and the evidence from wills of the vogue for building north aisles between 1532 and 1535,[1] might argue a date well on into the sixteenth century. There are few places in the county which exert such a fascination as this remote moorland church, which sits like a queen with her court ranged around her in widening circles. The closest of these is formed of Curry Mallet, Beer Crocombe, Ilton, Stocklinch, Kingsbury, Muchelney and Swell. Beyond and mostly on higher ground stand North Curry, Staple Fitzpaine, Ilminster, Shepton Beauchamp, Martock, Long Sutton, Huish Episcopi, Langport and Curry Rivel. Ile Abbots is the innermost shrine, the heart and core of so much beauty. Moreover, it is the most intact. Ten of its ancient statues still fill the higher niches of the perfect tower. The chancel, doubtless built by the monks of Muchelney, the owners of the church, survives from the thirteenth century. Windows, piscina, and sedilia are of an uncouth and primitive prettiness, thrown together without any connecting design. Yet more primitive and unexplained are the strange rustic symbols round the font. The rest, nave arcade, aisle and tower, were exquisitely rebuilt on the eve of the Reformation. The Laudian revival would seem to have added the grille-like screen under the tower, some of the benches, and the little doors to the fan-vaulted porch. How gladly would we lift here, as at Yatton, one corner from the past, see the stones rise, and hear the names of the builders! We must be content with an impersonal beauty. Around the base of the tower, beneath the Virgin and the Risen Christ, the lichen and the sunlight add ever new tones to the golden surface of the box tombs, the buttresses, the niches, the wall and the church-grass [36]. All else is the stillness of the centuries.[2]

4. TOWERS

The towers which rose up over the whole county in the last hundred and sixty years before the Reformation give a special glory to Somerset. They are more numerous, especially in the south, than anywhere in England, and they include a small group of peculiar excellence. Further, their

[1] See page 34.
[2] Three council houses, recently erected too close to the south have now intruded on this scene. Nor is a churchyard path in concrete to be commended.

interest, to an even greater extent than that of the churches in general, lies in their varied types: Dr. Allen, who insisted that he had given a lifetime to their study, enumerated eight groups, for the most part local, which he maintained had been made by as many schools of masons, besides many individual examples which refused such classification.[1] The eighth of these groups, that of West Somerset, is but part of the type which the intractable granite and sandstone made common over the whole south-west: there is nothing radically different between them and the bigger towers of Devon and Cornwall. From a distance they stand up well and strong and make their mark against the woods and the steep hills behind them, but on a closer view the slenderness of their buttresses, the sparsity of their windows and pinnacles, the lack of character in their tracery or parapets, render them monotonous and disappointing. The splendour of these churches lies in their carpentry (e.g. Minehead, Watchet, Norton Fitzwarren, Wellington).

The greater towers of the rest of the county have certain common characteristics: they will be found to have enough, if not all, of the following features to distinguish them from the rest of England or indeed of Europe: elaborate parapets; pinnacles in clusters, pinnacles of delicacy, pinnacles applied to the surface of pilasters or growing out of the upper stages of the buttresses, pinnacles set diagonally to the wall face or applied in half-section as pilasters themselves; canopied niches for statues which, alas, have mostly vanished; numerous heads and grotesques; 'Somerset tracery' instead of louvre boards in the windows; panelling continuing the window lines within their embrasures downward or to their sides, but not, as in Gloucestershire, overflowing to the wall surfaces outside; large west windows to light the interior of naves, which are often without clerestories; tower arches moulded or panelled on the interior; external stair turrets, usually in the north-east corner, rising above the parapet as a feature of the design. This last feature is common to the whole west, whereas in East Anglia and the Stamford area the stair casings are usually invisible from outside.

The first attempt to classify Somerset towers was made by Freeman as a young man in the first years of the Somerset Archaeological Society's existence. We have seen that in many respects, especially in his appreciation of the Perpendicular style, Freeman was ahead of his time. It is therefore all the more eloquent of the condition of taste and of architectural studies a hundred years ago that Freeman's extraordinary grouping of our towers according to the arrangement of their stair turret, a subordinate feature which is sometimes completely absent, should have been made by such a man and apparently generally accepted for fifty years. In 1904 Mr. R. P. Brereton, a master at Oundle, and Dr. Allen, to whom reference has already been made, working independently, had no difficulty in rejecting Freeman's

[1] F. J. Allen, *The Great Church Towers of England*, 1932.

39

thesis and proposed a new classification based in the main on the arrangement of the windows. Their papers were read at the same meeting at Gillingham; Mr. Brereton's was published in *The Archaeological Journal* and Dr. Allen's in the *Proceedings* for that year. Mr. Brereton died before the complete work which he contemplated could be published, but his illustrations for that book, issued on separate sheets, can still be bought at Taunton Castle.

Dr. Allen expanded his researches into *The Great Church Towers of England*, published in 1932, and died ten years later. The present author has drawn on both these pioneers for this study and especially on Dr. Allen's careful examination of individual towers. He has also used some of his photographs, taken some sixty years ago, which are often all the more interesting for that reason, as for instance those showing the old shambles at Shepton Mallet [40] or the condition of the tower at North Petherton before its restoration about 1909 [52]. As Allen's classification is now the most generally accepted and has passed into some of the guide books, we shall follow that where possible and only diverge from it where necessary. It must be realized that there is no documentary evidence for the theory of groups of masons in Somerset; it rests only on similarity of style. Moreover it has not been possible to find names for the designers such as Mr. Harvey has discovered or collated recently for so many other great buildings of the period. We may assume a probability, but not a certainty, that in the same district the same man designed towers whose belfries, for instance, had three windows rather than two, and whose parapets and buttresses were also similar. But similar features in districts wide apart carry much less conviction. Allen was very cautious in his dating and did not use even all the evidence to be found in wills: we shall take greater risks.

Allen's eight groups are as follows:

A	The Cathedral Group	E	The North Somerset
B	The West Mendip	F	The South Somerset
C	The Quantock Group	G	The Brislington
D	The East Mendip	H	The Devon

I Residual

It must be understood that these eight groups cover only the most important towers, some ninety in all, including the 'residuals'. The smaller and earlier or later towers are not included. They date from 1380 to 1540, except for the central tower of the cathedral, which was built about 1320. The latter, along with the Chapter House and Lady Chapel, form part of Dean Godelee's addition to the Early English fabric, and it is these notable Decorated constructions which still give Wells its picturesqueness from the east to-day. The tower was intended for a spire, but the support was inadequate, and the great inverted arches within had to be built instead. It thus became inadvertently one of the earliest towers with a flat roof, for earlier types had first been topped with saddle backs like the example at Swainswick [10], or pyramidal caps like those in St. Joseph's Chapel at Glastonbury, and then with spires. When it was found that the ornate Decorated towers looked well without a spire, the type remained and has been the normal receptacle for bells ever since. Peals of bells became popular at this time, and the practical function of the tower was to house them; the purpose of the belfry windows was to release their sound. Local pride, the spirit of rivalry, the good local stone and craftsmanship, and the genius of art did the rest.

The chief feature of the central tower of Wells [37] is three tall compartments on each face of the upper chamber, separated by bold shafts, and each formed of two lights continued downwards to the next stage in the form of panels: thus, each compartment and light, despite transoms, seems to continue as one long window and member through both top stages. A far-off echo of this design is at Ilminster [19] built nearly two hundred years later (c. 1500). In the interval it had been responsible for the south-west tower of the cathedral built in 1386, the north-west tower copied from it in 1424, St. Cuthbert's (c. 1430) [18a], Wrington (1420–50) [38], Evercreech [39] and Batcombe [44], successively later. The pinnacles are richer and the ogee tracery more developed at Evercreech than at Wrington; Batcombe is yet further developed, and should be compared with Chewton Mendip [45] which also has a very similar composition of sculpture on its west face. These towers all have large panelled windows, and their similarity, particularly in those of St. Cuthbert's, Wrington, and Evercreech is obvious and striking. Yet Allen confined his own 'Cathedral' group to the Cathedral and St. Cuthbert's, placed Evercreech and Batcombe in 'East Mendip' (along with Weston Zoyland, Bruton [Frontispiece] and Leigh [34a], and Wrington in 'North Somerset' (along with Yeovil [14a] and Backwell [43]. I cannot follow him in this, for his reasons are unconvincing. For instance, he adduces five features at Wrington which differ from his 'North Somerset' group and are derived from Wells (string-courses not carried round the buttresses, long panels and corner pinnacles, pilasters between the windows continuing through the parapet, parapets perforated with trefoils), and only two which differ from Wells (the shape of the buttresses and the corners of the towers, which are like Blagdon or Publow, and the trefoils in the parapet, which are like those at Portishead or Banwell). The first of these two differences is obscure and the other trifling, yet he considers them the more important and groups Wrington accordingly.

The western towers of the cathedral have massive outstanding buttresses dictated by the position of the Early English work below, and these tend to obscure the long panels of the windows, but the design first introduced in Bishop Harewell's tower in 1386 is continued in these four towers for perhaps a hundred years, by which time elaborate pinnacles and other features have been added to it. So few examples over so long an interval are, indeed, no argument for a school of masons, but they prove the local persistence in North Somerset of a noble idea which prevails over all other features of the design and suffices to link them together in the mind of their admirers.

Dr. Allen is doubtless right in attaching great importance to the tower of his native town of Shepton Mallet [40], which he dates at about 1380. The grounds for this date are by no means clearly stated, but in my opinion it can nevertheless be accepted. The tower's chief interest is that it was obviously designed for a spire, which, indeed, was completed to a height of eight feet and then covered by a lead cap. The upper stage of this tower is greatly set back, to this purpose, and the buttress heads with their pinnacles project a great way from the tower angles in consequence. It is very likely that Wedmore [16a] and Axbridge [17a], which were probably derived from Shepton Mallet, were also once intended for spires. This alone, as well as their central position, would indicate an early date. Allen regards Shepton as the prototype for the 'West Mendip' group and for others as well. This group is certainly so local and its towers so similar in style that we may be sure they were designed by the same man. Its common features are three windows in the top stage, one in each of the lower stages, straight parapets, shallow buttresses, and the local grey stone. The picture of Wedmore or Axbridge, though these towers are central, will serve also for the western tower of Banwell, Cheddar, Winscombe, Weare, Mark, Bleadon, and South Brent[1]. Their differences are too slight to mention: together they form the most homogeneous group in the county. We may put their date at about 1380–1440.

To the influence of Shepton Mallet, Dr. Allen also attributed a group of nine towers which he calls the 'East Mendip', of which he thinks Bruton [Frontispiece], probably built between 1450 and 1490, the earliest. This may put its birth a hundred years after that of its parent, a feat of fertility which would only be credible if the family likeness, as at Cranmore, were indeed so striking. But it is not. The added height of the triple top windows, the greater shallowness of the buttresses, the battlemented crest, and the increase of pinnacles and niches have altered the whole balance of the design and introduced something more handsome and more graceful. However, in the absence of evidence of other parentage some influence from Shepton may be admitted, along with many features which may come from the south or from farther afield. The design of Bruton is further developed in the noblest of the northern towers, that of Leigh-on-Mendip

[1] South Brent is an alternative name to Brent Knoll.

[34a], and also at Mells, which is very similar but less ornate. In both of these there are triple windows in both the upper stages, but the battlements at Mells sadly need a richer treatment. It is a sound aesthetic principle which demands an increase in decoration towards the higher parts of buildings, and this is nowhere more obvious than in towers. Cranmore is an obvious copy of Shepton, from which it is distant only three miles: it has the same heavy buttresses, the same upper story, the same cone-topped stair turret, all on a smaller scale, though the panelled tower arches and the four-centred west door may show that it was made a century later. Dr. Allen claims that Weston Zoyland, far away on Sedgemoor, through its resemblance to Bruton, and also its neighbour Middlezoy, belongs to this class. But here again his own evidence tells against him and grotesquely so in the case of Middlezoy, where he enumerates six or seven Quantock features and hardly any from the east. On the other hand he excludes Chewton [45] which has strong affinities to Leigh and Mells. Here, too, the belfry stage, though only of two windows, is repeated blind in the second stage, and below it is the same sculptured group as at Batcombe, where Our Lord in glory is attended by three pairs of angels (censers above, the ladder, the nails and the crown in the middle, scrolls and feathered legs for the seraphim below). We have seen that Batcombe and Chewton were being made at the same time, 1540-1. Chewton is the tallest of the village towers; it measures 119 feet to the top of the pinnacles, whereas most are from 80 to a 100 feet.[1]

This leaves very little of the 'East Mendip' group. One small tower, Cranmore, is acknowledged as the legitimate offspring of Shepton Mallet, Bruton may have some indirect relationship, but Leigh and Mells have become a distinct species. Evercreech belongs to Wells, Weston Zoyland and Middlezoy to the Quantocks, Batcombe is a healthy mongrel with obvious relationship to Chewton. Nunney is insignificant. What remains hardly constitutes a family. There are four or five fine towers in the east Mendips; that is all that we can say.

The chief feature of Allen's next group, 'North Somerset', is the strongly marked horizontal division of its four stages, the string-course being continued round the buttresses as in Gloucestershire, and the tower angles being left exposed between them. The parapet is straight and frequently arcaded. Chew Magna is the type of this class. Variations occur at Dundry, where the over-heavy crown seems to have been imported bodily from Gloucestershire, and at Backwell, where the top stage was happily altered after a storm in the seventeenth century and a striking and original feature was introduced—that of an enclosing ogee hood rising through the parapet [43].

---

[1] Of the town towers, Taunton is 163 feet, St. Cuthbert's 142, Glastonbury 134, St. James's, Taunton, 111—figures from Brereton.

Others in this class are Winford, Batheaston, Publow, perhaps Blagdon, Portishead, and the Temple Church at Bristol which, like St. Mary Redcliffe, lies within Somerset. For various reasons we must reject Dr. Allen's inclusion of Yeovil, Wrington, and Lympsham. The rest are a fairly homogeneous but undistinguished group. They probably date from the first part of the fifteenth century, but Dundry, which was placed very conspicuously on a hill 750 feet up by the Merchant Adventurers of Bristol, contains a stone dated 1482. They are not markedly of a Somerset type.

The chief features of Dr. Allen's seventh group, 'Brislington', seem to be a spire or spirelet and 'refinement of detail', qualities which are vague in the extreme. It consists of the scattered churches of Brislington, Croscombe, Chew Stoke, Tickenham, Binegar, and Wookey. The churches are unimportant and 'the group' carries no conviction. If groups must be formed in this region, I should consider a more convincing and attractive one would be made of the little churches of Weston, Stanton Prior, and Farmborough, with their same grey stone, similar two-light windows in the top story, angle pinnacles and turret.

There are, however, five churches in South Somerset whose towers have an unmistakable similarity. These are Norton-sub-Hamdon [42], Crewkerne [17b], Curry Rivel, Shepton Beauchamp, and Hinton St. George. Each one has a very tall window extending through both upper stages and divided by a thick ornamented transom. Below is a large space without windows. From each of the eight buttresses rises a triangular pilaster which terminates in a pinnacle on either side of each tower angle. They share this feature with some of the chief Dorset churches, such as Fordington and Piddletrenthide. Thus these five towers have one broad effect and one significant detail in common. At Crewkerne the tower is central. Shepton Beauchamp violates the principle mentioned above by putting its wealth on the ground floor and its poverty in the skies, but it contains a superb west window, whose effect inside is now unfortunately spoilt by a fine modern organ on a tall loft which masks one half of it.

We have left to the last that Somerset tower *par excellence* which Allen has called the Quantock tower. The name is not strictly accurate, for true examples are found only south and east of those hills, and three of the finest are far away in the moors, but it will stand for want of a better; new nomenclatures will only make confusion. Brereton called it the Taunton Deane type, and it is probable that the masons came from Taunton, the chief town in the neighbourhood. There can be little disagreement about its characteristics or its chief components; uncertainty can exist only about its origins or outliers. The chief towers are, in their probable chronological order: Bishop's Lydeard and Taunton St. James; Ile Abbots, Staple Fitzpaine, and Kingston; Kingsbury, Huish Episcopi, and North Petherton;

Taunton St. Mary; Probus in Cornwall and Chittlehampton in north Devon. Other towers in the same area with affinities to the group are, in order of importance: Middlezoy, Chedzoy and Lyng, Martock and Ruishton, Hatch Beauchamp and St. Benignus, Glastonbury. Weston Zoyland, Langport, Long Sutton, and Muchelney stand somewhat apart; their lias formation is more prominent than their Ham Hill dressings. The influence of the group can be seen at Ilminster in its own country and at Bruton and Batcombe some way beyond it. It can also be traced in other more modest structures.

The characteristics of the group are wealth and delicacy of detail; rich battlemented crowns; exuberance of pinnacles; frequent niches, gargoyles, and heads; bands of quatrefoils; pierced stone-work in the windows, i.e. Somerset tracery; a predominance of ogee curves; two windows in the top story; good proportions. Finally all the carved work in the Somerset churches is in Ham Hill stone. All these features will be found in the best examples; some of them in all. Only at Kingsbury and Martock in this group is the whole tower of Ham Hill stone—both building material and dressings. At Bishop's Lydeard and the two Taunton churches (both rebuilt in the nineteenth century) the building material is the local red sandstone: at Ile Abbots the west face is of Ham Hill, the rest of blue lias. Even more than their style, the fine golden stone of their dressings is the link between all these churches: it is the link also with other local churches of different styles such as Norton, Shepton Beauchamp, Hinton St. George, Crewkerne, Ilminster, Montacute, and Sherborne Abbey, which are entirely built of Ham Hill stone.

Dr. Allen may be right in considering Bishop's Lydeard [41] the ancestor of the group and in claiming that it too, was begotten of Shepton Mallet. A comparison shows four similar stages in each, but here, as at Bruton, in the course of fifty years or so something much more elegant and accomplished has been evolved. The buttresses are more slender, battlements have taken the place of the northern type of crown, Somerset tracery and pinnacles have increased, the ogee arches in the window lights have added a delicate rhythm to the whole movement. Taunton St. James is an almost identical design but some twelve feet taller (120 feet): a different crown was added at the otherwise faithful reconstruction in 1870, but this did not affect the height.

From these two, which we may perhaps date at about 1440-50, it is a shorter step to three smaller towers which also are so alike that they must have had the same architect. Their measurements are within a few feet the same, their height being just over 80 feet, the disposition of the windows, pinnacles and niches is the same. There is a mastery and beauty of design in the towers of Ile Abbots [47], Staple Fitzpaine, and Kingston [49] which renders them among the greatest masterpieces of English architecture. The reduction to three stages, a greater proportion of freestone, and a relatively longer and more independent crown distinguish them from Bishop's Lydeard and might place their date at between 1480 and 1490. The differences between them are subtle and interesting, and might determine the order of their building. Thus at Ile Abbots the space between the windows and the crown might well be thought on completion to be too great, and the ogee is not used in the window lights of the upper stages. We might therefore assume that this was built first. At Kingston the windows are improved by weather mouldings, and the flying shafts to the corner pinnacles, which become more prominent later, have appeared. Kingston therefore is the perfected model. The difference in tone between the blue and the red foundations can be appreciated even in the photographs. If Ile Abbots can still charm the most, this may be because of its remoter setting, a more beautiful church below, and the survival of no less than ten of its original statues. On the west side are the Blessed Virgin and the Resurrection, St. Peter, and St. Paul. On the east is St. John the Baptist with the Agnus Dei in his hand, and St. Clement with papal tiara, double cross, and anchor. On the south side are St. Margaret, St. Katharine, and St. George. On the north the Archangel Michael.

Kingsbury, Huish, and North Petherton are a third clearly-related family. Though of the normal height for the more important Somerset towers— about 100 feet—they have kept the three stages of the last group. The most obvious change is the introduction of bands of quatrefoils to accentuate the string-courses. At Kingsbury [34b] and at Huish [50] the flying pinnacles have become more prominent; they have been wisely eliminated at North Petherton [52, 53]. At Kingsbury the buttresses are too shallow, have been placed too far from the tower angles, and cease before the last stage; the result is that the pinnacles resting on them do not appear in the outline when the tower is seen diagonally; further the plain part below the battlements is too wide. These factors render the crown far too heavy, and vitiate the design. In all these towers, some of the windows have tracery of the Midland type where the mullions run straight into the arch: in the more attractive Somerset type they curve, and latterly into ogees, before meeting it. Another foreign influence, from Gloucestershire, may be seen at Petherton; the whole space between the upper windows and the crown is panelled, which greatly adds to the general splendour. In other respects, too, this design is the grandest in the county; the string-courses are continued round the buttresses. The horizontal and the vertical lines are again happily balanced, as they were in the Ile Abbots group. The whole concept is organic and superb.

Clearly these three towers are later in date than the last three. On stylistic grounds we might allow some thirty years for the development, and place them between 1510 and 1520. Two pieces of documentary evidence support a late date. The tower of Probus in Cornwall, though built of the intractable local stone, is evidently a close imitation of Petherton. A law suit was brought by the parishioners before the Star Chamber about the year 1517 to restrain a local landowner from hindering the building of the church.[1] Nicholas Carminowe and his wife boasted that they would make the Probus men beg their bread before they should build the tower, and forcibly prevented their doing so by setting their servants on them 'with swords, bucklers, bills, and short dags [daggers]'. Carminowe's motive may have been Protestantism, but it is more likely, especially in so Catholic a district, to have been his wife's jealousy of her elder sister, who had inherited most of her father's property, but shared the quarry. The judgment of the court is not given, but the tower was built. It is arguable, therefore, that the tower of North Petherton was built shortly before 1517: the Cornishmen are unlikely to have wanted to copy something so far away, unless it was 'the latest thing'.[2] On the other hand that work of this type was being done as late as 1530–3 we have seen from the fact that money was left at that time to build the little tower of Ruishton, whose completion was doubtless interrupted by the Reformation. It still stands sadly without its crown. All this would put Kingsbury and Huish at between 1500 and 1510.

There remains the tower of St. Mary Magdalene at Taunton, which can be dated with greater certainty than any others [51]. Wills published by the Somerset Record Society show no fewer than twelve bequests to the new tower of 'Mawdelyn', or 'Maudelon' or 'Magdeleyn' church (there is delightful variation in the spelling.[3]) In 1486 Walter Eston left a number of gifts to the church but makes no mention of new building or of the tower. In 1488 this begins and continues till 1514 when William Nethway left 26s. 8d. to the 'Katerynke of two wyndowes in the tower' (this probably means the tracery or Somerset tracery, for 'cater' meant to cut diagonally); in 1503 'half a pippe of oode' ($\frac{1}{4}$ ton of woad) is left for the finishing of the tower, and directions are given for glazing its 'gabull windows'. Besides, many bequests in money, gifts of cloth, woad and iron ('a hoge head', a $\frac{1}{4}$ ton in 1505) are bequeathed and show the class and occupation of the donors. It might be expected that wills would furnish more evidence about the building of other towers and churches, but those quoted in this book seem to exhaust all that has so far been revealed from this source. There are

[1] The document is undated, but it states that they had been quarrying peacefully for three years in the accustomed place when Carminowe, one of the joint owners, suddenly forbade its use. He had inherited a share in the quarry from his father-in-law, John Wolvedun, whose death in 1514 is attested by a brass in the church.

[2] *Journal of the Royal Institution of Cornwall*, vol. ix, 1889.

[3] S.R.S., xvi, pp. 264, 279; xix, p. 53.

of course innumerable gifts to parish churches of small sums, but these are given generally, and few make specific reference to new buildings. In the villages the farmer leaves his cows and sheep, besides money and household goods, to the church, just as the townsman leaves his merchandise. It is also interesting to find that a small gift to the 'modern church of Wells' is very frequent, and that countrymen made bequests to neighbouring churches besides their own (e.g. in 1523 William Mede of Corymalet, 'hosbondman, leaves 20d. to each of the churches of Hach Becham, Bere Crokam, and Ile Abbots' as well as to his own).

Taunton rises to 163 feet; it is the largest and most splendid of our towers, but it is not the most beautiful [51]. This cannot be ascribed to its complete rebuilding from the ground in 1862, for the work was faithfully done: the original design and detail were exactly reproduced, though possibly in a redder stone than the original. It is the gradations and proportions which were ill-managed. Features from too many sources have been combined. The lower stages of double windows from the Mendip churches, panelling above the top windows, like North Petherton, from the Temple church at Bristol, and a crown from Gloucester, where the tower had been made in 1460–70. All these, together with buttresses of insufficient offset, have been imposed on features of the Quantock type, and the result, though impressive, fails to give the unalloyed pleasure afforded by the five or six previous examples.

Among the towers which have not fallen into any of our classifications we must confine ourselves to two at Glastonbury. St. John's [18b] comes fitly after Taunton, for it, too, is of unusual size (134 feet) and is of even more alien origin than Taunton. The crown, the panelling, the heavy string-course are all from Gloucestershire, but we shall not refuse the neighbouring county our tribute of admiration for the presence of so handsome a stranger in our midst. As we have seen, it was probably built between 1460 and 1490. An emblem of all our towers, though not especially characteristic of the style of any one of them, is St. Michael's on the Tor, built about 1400 near the site of a chapel destroyed in a landslide [46]. Its church has disappeared, and the tower is a mere shell without any special architectural merit, but it is better known and closer to the hearts of the people of Somerset than any other. From all sides and from many unexpected places it meets the eye; as one descends the hills from the east and the north, it is the first thing in the landscape; it rises 500 hundred feet above the surrounding moors and dominates them from the foothills to the sea; it looks over the shoulders of the low central ridges, and is prominent from Blackdown, the Quantocks, and the Brendons far away to the west. To those with an historical sense it is a perpetual reminder of the great abbey at its feet which lay there, venerated, mysterious, and powerful, for over a thousand years; and it recalls the fatal day when the last of its abbots fell a victim to Leviathan, the eternal enemy. To destroy so great an influence there was made so brutal an example. From that day no more fine towers were built in Somerset.

5. ROOFS

After the towers the roofs—and here we must take second place to East Anglia and even expect a challenge from Cheshire and North Wales. Somerset has only three roofs of the very front rank—Shepton Mallet, Martock and Somerton—which may compare with the hammerbeams of the east: the hammerbeam is unknown in the west. Our churches show three main types: (1) The arch-braced or wagon roof, whose structure is usually concealed by plaster. (2) The tie-beam roof with king-posts. (3) The flat roof supported by cambered or furred beams. There is also an unusual type, here and elsewhere, which should first be noticed. This is the double-framed couple roof of Hinton St. George, whose dangerous thrust is only counteracted by the strength of its aisles [54a]. A tie-beam, a brace, or a collar are the means normally adopted to overcome this difficulty. All these means were in use well before the fifteenth century, but it is difficult or impossible, except in a few cases such as Martock, to date our roofs with exactitude. Plaster or frequent subsequent repairs often conceal the original structure. They were naturally made after the walls on which they rest, but nothing is more natural than that some of the earlier timber should be used again in reconstructions. The tendency of the later Middle Ages was to make roofs of a lower pitch. The line of an earlier roof may be seen in the courses of the tower at North Curry [11b] or Northover [64a], St. Cuthbert's Wells [18a], and in many other places, and it is invariably steeper. We may assume then that apart from the re-use of old material few of our roofs will date from before the late Perpendicular period, that the best of them date from then, but that because of the nature of their material many of them have since been altered or lost. The seventeenth century repaired or rebuilt on medieval lines, despite an original surface decoration as at Muchelney, East Brent or Axbridge; the eighteenth century ceiled and plastered in a comfortably domestic style, as at Bruton or Spaxton; the Victorians made new roofs which are usually easily recognizable, for although they aped the Middle Ages, they disregarded the local practice and introduced inferior material. For example, there is a false hammerbeam at Bridgwater, scissor beams (a rare type in the Middle Ages) at Edington and Skilgate, and a school piece with collars, tie-beams, king-posts and very long wall posts at Combe St. Nicholas, most of them in imported fir. The material of the medieval roof was always oak.

We will now take the three main types in order: (1) The construction of the single-framed wagon roof is well seen in the early fifteenth-century example at Halse, which lies open for most of its length [54b]. The braces supporting each pair of rafters and their collar form a series of arches which when boarded and ceiled produce the commonest type of old roof in the county. In the double-framed type such as the choir of Queen Camel [22], the chief weight is taken by the principals, and the rafters between them are largely supported by the purlins running from east to west; bosses cover their intersection. It was common to give special treatment to the parts of the roof above the rood or the altar, and the section ceiled at Halse may have been thus designed; the crucifix once stood where a rood beam has been replaced in this century. Originally this part would have been painted, perhaps in the manner still to be seen at Muchelney, to represent a starry sky [73]. As at Halse, slender ribs were applied in the manner of purlins and principals to the under surface of the single-framed sort for merely decorative purposes, and here again decorative bosses are placed at the intersections. At Congresbury these are unusually large and square, and show heads and foliage of great boldness of design.[1] At Queen Camel the monks of Cleeve, the patrons of the church, displayed on a roof very similar to that of their own refectory the popular stories of the medieval bestiary in all their quaintness and *naïveté*. Here is the great sea turtle, Aspido Chelone, type of the devil, so vast that mariners mistake him for an island and are lured to their death; the undying Phoenix, type of Christ's Resurrection; the Eagle, type of his Ascension, who flies towards the sun; the Virgin and the Unicorn, type of his Nativity, for the unicorn may only be caught while resting in a virgin's lap; the Elephant and Castle, the man-eating Mantichora, the Amphisbaena, the Basilisk, and many others of that company.[2]

The most remarkable wagon roof in the county, or indeed anywhere, is at Shepton Mallet [60]. Its structure, which is of the ordinary single-frame type described above, is completely concealed. The three hundred and fifty panels, each one of different design, are carved in rows on planks which are nailed to the arch braces; the massive ribs with their foliated bosses, each with its four attendant leaves beneath it, are nailed to the panels. Far from supporting the roof, which is the illusion they give, they are supported by it. On each side, upon and beneath the cornice, eighteen angels spread their wings. This marvellous work would appear to have been executed about 1500.[3] It may be doubted whether the square panel motif is not more

---

[1] Illustrations in C. J. P. Cave, *Roof Bosses*, Cambridge, 1948.

[2] They were discovered, elucidated and photographed by Miss Bennett of Sparkford, G. C. Druce, and C. J. P. Cave.

[3] F. J. Allen in P 1907.

suited, aesthetically, to the flat or king-post roof where it is more usually found, but it must be recognized that the work at Shepton Mallet is a stupendous *tour de force*. Structurally it is very bold, for all this weight must exert a great thrust on the three arches on each side of the nave and on the inadequate flat aisle roofs beyond them.

In West Somerset these wagon roofs are especially finely carved: a rich trellis runs along the wall plates and is relieved, as at Watchet [56] and in the beautiful church of Selworthy [57], by an array of shield-bearing angels. Wootton Courtney, Sampford Brett, Old Cleeve, and Dunster are other examples. They take up again, as at Broomfield [32], the leafy pattern and intertwining tendrils of the capitals and benches.

(2) The finest of Somerset roofs are the tie-beams of low pitch holding short king-posts, and supported by wall posts springing from between the clerestory windows. The principals hold three purlins, including the ridge purlin, and these, with the subsidiary ribs, form a series of diminishing squares which give great scope for a variety of ornament. The triangles formed by the tie-beams and the principals are also richly adorned; angels face east and west at the feet of the king-posts or stand with outspread wings along the cornices. The tie-beams themselves are often battlemented and richly moulded, and decorated with rosettes on a slender trellis. Bosses of rich foliage cover the intersection of the members. Finally, in the richest, most sub-divided examples, which are Somerton and Martock, the dominant motif comes from scores of little square panels filled with quatre-foils and other geometrical patterns. These two are, with Shepton Mallet, incomparably the finest roofs in the county, but their panels do not show the same fertile invention. At Martock, where a shield with the date 1513 survives, there are but six patterns in all, one for each bay, a hundred and twenty-eight panels in each bay, total seven hundred and sixty-eight [58]. At Somerton there are also a hundred and twenty-eight panels in each bay, but only five bays, total six hundred and forty, and the pattern is the same in each panel [59]. It is a curious thing that the dimensions of each roof are almost identical (about 87 by 31 feet), but as there are only five bays at Somerton to six at Martock, the panels at Somerton must be slightly larger and those at Martock, perhaps not quite square. It provides a nice problem in arithmetic. At Martock the triangles are filled with a pattern of quatre-foils set in lozenges in the manner of the parapets of Axbridge and the northern group of towers. At Somerton these triangles, which are flatter, hold the twenty-two monsters which are the most striking feature of the church. The cornice at Martock has been unfeelingly renewed at a later date; that at Somerton is richly decorated and intact. On the other hand the roof at Somerton is not related to the windows nor so closely suited to the design of the church; the sparseness of openings in the clerestory may render

the walls strong enough to support the tie-beams without the aid of corbels and wall posts. The roof at Martock has an organic connection with the church and is flooded with light from twelve noble windows. Architecturally it is the most satisfactory of the three, but many will prefer the mysterious gloom of the little grey town on the hill-top, where the dragons, growing larger towards the east, prowl and gnash their great teeth in the shadows and the carpenter has permitted himself a few rare freaks of fancy.[1]

The other roofs of this type are not so ornate, but many of them have excellent proportions. Among the best of these is Weston Zoyland [25].[2] Others are at Long Sutton [24], High Ham [55], Bruton, Pilton, Leigh-on-Mendip, East Pennard [61], North Cadbury [23], Queen Camel [22], and Wellow. At Wellow the triangles are filled with flat panels on which an archer and other figures stand up in relief. Two angels swinging censers have survived in paint above the rood at East Pennard. Less satisfactory is the roof at St. Cuthbert's Wells: the beams are richly cusped above and below, but they stand out too lavishly against the relative simplicity of the intervening spaces, and the same criticism may be applied to Taunton.

(3) There remain the flat roofs, supported by beams cambered or furred enough to permit the rain to drain off the leads which were increasingly used as a roofing material at the end of the Middle Ages. Such roofs were naturally mostly employed on the shorter spans; it was dangerous to rest the big roofs on the beams alone. This was sometimes done, however; the nave roofs at Wrington and North Petherton are flat, but the best examples are in aisles, transepts, or porches. There is one painted with angels over an aisle at Wedmore, and a particularly elaborate example over the north transept at Crewkerne. This was only half completed and thus shows the method of construction; each panel holds a quatrefoil with a shield set at different angles within it; these and the north-south ribs have been made in the whole roof, but in the northern part of it the east-west ribs which would complete the squares along with their attendant foliage were perhaps still to come when the Reformation arrested the work. The finest aisle roofs are at Keynsham, Mark, and South Brent [62]. The two latter are only three miles apart and are so similar that they must have been made by the same carpenter at the same time, probably in the first decade of the sixteenth century, or later. Moreover, they have the same shields and leaf decoration which may be seen at Crewkerne. At Mark, both in the aisles and the porch, the same patterns recur on a regular plan; here and at Keynsham

[1] A barrel may be seen in the top left-hand corner of the photograph; there is a lion's head farther east, and many leafy variations in the bosses.
[2] Well restored by Mr. Caroe and through the zeal of its vicar, the Rev. G. M. Evans, between 1933 and 1938.

there are some six to ten different patterns in each.[1] The roof at South Brent is the finer, for it has greater variations. Its ninety-six panels are never repeated: the style and ingenuity of their patterns recalls Shepton Mallet, and though I have been unable to find any of the Shepton patterns reproduced here, there can be little doubt that they are from the same workshop. On the other hand the panels at Martock and Somerton seem each to have had a separate origin; their styles differ from each other and also from the Shepton Mallet group.

6. SCREENS AND OTHER FITTINGS

At the Reformation almost every church possessed a screen to mark the division between nave and chancel, to act in some cases as a pedestal for the rood, and above all to support a loft where musicians accompanied the service from a point of vantage. The destruction of these lofts, ordered in 1561, was a Protestant move against the popular church music under cover of an attack on superstition: but what superstition, when the roods themselves had already been destroyed in 1548? Anyhow it was duly carried out in most of the country, and so thoroughly that no lofts have survived in Somerset. Weston Zoyland shows one of modern design erected on the old screen about 1937 [25]. The remoteness of Wales, and perhaps the invincible love of music of its people, has saved many of its magnificent lofts, and it is there, and in a few examples in Devonshire which survive for the same reason, that the type may now be seen in its most perfect form. Although there was no legal order for the removal of the remaining part of the screens, these gradually disappeared, and never so rapidly as in the middle of the last century, under the strangest of influences. It was then the object of high churchmen to restore the importance of the altar, and to render it visible and accessible to the whole congregation. In this respect the screen was an encumbrance and was therefore removed; it was an obstacle to that thorough 'restoration' which has left its mark everywhere. In the intervening period it had been the principle of Anglican worship to keep each part of the church for its proper function: the parson sat in the nave for Morning and Evening Prayer and the congregation sat in the chancel for the Communion. Consequently, although many screens were undoubtedly destroyed in the eighteenth century, the majority were retained.[2]

In Somerset the earliest surviving examples seem to date from the end of the fourteenth century (e.g. Culbone and the aisle at Dunster), but most

[1] Despite two drastic restorations, first after the fall of the tower in 1632, and then in Victorian times, most of the panels of the north aisle seem still to be original. See below, p. 69.
[2] G. W. O. Addleshaw and F. Etchells, *The Architectural Setting of Anglican Worship*, p. 37. Aymer Vallance, *English Church Screens*, pp. 25, 91.

from the great epoch of church building on the eve of the Reformation. The greatest of them all, which spans the whole width of the nave and aisles, was built in 1499 at Dunster after a dispute and a legal decision which separated the monastic and the parochial church. It is in consequence far to the westward of the normal position. There is evidence that some of these screens were carved in Exeter,[1] and there is also evidence which shows that the art was within the powers of the village carpenter, after visits to various models. Thus at Yatton the parish bore the expense of journeys to Easton-in-Gordano to see the 'alle' (alure or gallery) there, and then to Selwood Forest to buy the wood.[2] The influence of Devonshire, where the richest and most numerous examples are still to be found, is thus conclusively proved. But it needs no such proof. The screen, like the tower, the roofs, the arcades and the landscape, proclaim the affinities of west Somerset with its western neighbour. To these we may add the plan of the building itself. The normal Devon church has no structural division between nave and chancel, the wagon roof runs continuously through both with no chancel arch. To this type many churches in west Somerset conform, e.g. Minehead, Selworthy, Porlock, Dulverton. Our screens lie thickest on the soil in the west, and are there of the Devonshire type, long, relatively low, fan-vaulted and canopied, adorned with long projecting cornices to hold the loft with its vanished balconies. Of these the best besides Dunster [63a] are at Minehead, Withycombe, Carhampton, Halse [54b], Fitzhead, Timberscombe, Bicknoller, Norton Fitzwarren, Trull, and Bishop's Lydeard.

Screens were portable and not dependent on geology; their influence naturally extended farther east than that of the other western features, and for that reason it is not possible to draw that firm line of demarcation which is so evident in the towers. The type extends sporadically as far east as High Ham [55], Long Sutton [24] and Queen Camel [22], and as far north as Banwell [63b]. All these are particularly fine; they are all arched and fan-vaulted. The more native type in north-east Somerset, however, is that of the Midlands generally. Its bressummer rests, as those of the west cannot do, on the nave walls; its panels are square-headed; it is designed, as the chancel arch dictates, separately for aisle and nave, so that the rood screen may be higher than those of the aisles. The late Bligh Bond, in studying the type,[3] traced its development through a hundred years by the pattern of the tracery heads. Of these he found the earliest at Nunney at the beginning

---

[1] Pilton in 1508, Elworthy, and a former screen at Croscombe. P 1907, p. 86. S.R.S., iv, pp. 55, 74.

[2] S.R.S., iv, p. 86.

[3] P 1905-8. See also P 1905 for Banwell, of which full details exist in the Wardens' Accounts: the screen was made between 1520 and 1525, the first entry being for paper to draw the draft, 4d.

of the fifteenth century, the last at Pilton, where the Churchwardens' Accounts date it to between 1498 and 1508. Part of the Pilton rood-screen is now at North Cheriton, but a parclose screen remains. In the interval come successively specimens of various importance, at Backwell, West Pennard, Congresbury, Wellow, Priddy, and Mells. Of these Congresbury and Wellow are the best, but the finest is at Long Ashton which extends across the whole church and has certain features in common with the west. The aisle screen at Keynsham is particularly rich and attractive, with coved head decorated with little stars but without fan-vaulting.

The inspiration for the best work certainly came from the west, but its effect is to my mind most satisfactory when set in the architectural frame-work of churches of the Somerset type such as Long Sutton or High Ham. The Devonshire type of church, which is one long low unbroken axis bisected artificially, and without any organic connexion with the structure, by a long low elaboration of woodwork, is aesthetically disturbing. It is pretty rather than noble. At High Ham the vertical lines predominate and lead the eye upward to the handsome roofs instead of sideways into the wall surfaces [55]. Apart from general design, the delicacy and fancy of the carving, as in all woodwork, is a chief reason for delight. The ever-recurrent vine trellis, the rope-strung leaves, or the dragon legend of Norton Fitz-warren,[1] will always please. On a tympanum board which survives at Win-sham, there are the very faint traces of a painted rood; apart from this there is none of the fine figure painting of East Anglia or the coarser work of Devonshire in our churches. Some decorative paint may still be seen in places, but it has not always been well treated by posterity. Carhampton (1862), Timberscombe, and Long Sutton [24] are examples of new paint in varying degrees unwisely applied.[2]

Somerset has a further very fine display of woodwork in its benches and pulpits. A few benches, including some at Mark and at Clapton-in-Gor-dano, rude and low and with curved ends, may date from the thirteenth century, but the greater part of them come from the end of our great epoch. By then it had become customary to provide seating in the naves as well as in the choirs, and from this epoch well over a thousand survive. We can mention here only some of the most typical or the most interest-ing.

Some, like those at East Brent [75] and South Brent or North Cadbury [23], have a simple form of poppy-head.[3] More often, and invariably in west Somerset, the ends are square. On these the medieval carpenter made a wide range of patterns and devices, architectural, natural, and human.

---

[1] A. W. Vivian-Neal discusses this legend in *N. & Q.*, xxii, p. 245.
[2] F. Bligh Bond in P 1906, p. 67.
[3] So-called from the stern, or 'puppis', of a ship.

Some, in their mullions and tracery, as at Thornfalcon, reflect the style of the windows; others, as at Broomfield, reach a high standard of decorative design. As we approach the wilder country of the south and west, the hunting scenes become irresistible; rabbits, hounds, and stags leap among the leaves; a man is shooting birds with a bow at Barwick, a dog has a rabbit by the tail at Monksilver, there is a dragon-killer at Crowcombe. At Lyng there are wrestlers and a charming courting scene. At Trull there is a whole procession, now unfortunately scattered about the church: candle bearer, cross bearer, subdeacon, deacon, and priest on successive benches, so rudely carved as almost to appear burlesques by Protestants. The windmills and ships at Bishop's Lydeard are well known, and so is the fuller at Spaxton. As surely as the rolls of cloth which stand by a kneeling man and a woman on a boss at Croscombe, he proclaims the economic origin of all this work. At East Brent may be seen the Cross with the Virgin and Child in the first quarter, which are the arms of Glastonbury, the symbols of the four Evangelists, and other sacred subjects. Over the hill at South Brent an incipient Protestantism can be scented in the famous satire of the Abbot-fox. Some of these benches, as we have seen, bear dates and the names of the carvers. The latest of them take on a distinctly Renaissance character, as in the figures and heads at Churchstanton, Nettlecombe, Milverton, and North Cadbury. The work is continued under the Catholic reaction; Mary's initial and the date 1559 appear at Chedzoy, but it may be too fanciful to see her kneeling figure at Milverton, accompanied by Bishop Gardiner and Cardinal Pole; another head nearby has an uncomfortable resemblance to her father, yet another bears his arms, and the date 1540 is on the screen.

The prettiest wooden pulpits of this time are at Monksilver and Chedzoy, the richest at Trull and Long Sutton [24]. Others of more conventional window design are at Bridgwater, Bruton, North Petherton, Queen Camel [22], and Somerton. There are wooden lecterns at Cheddar, Chedzoy, High Ham, and Wedmore. Somerset has two of the twenty-one wooden eagles in England, at East Brent and at Monksilver.

There is a brass eagle at Huish Champflower, and a brass lectern at Yeovil of similar design and date to that in Eton College Chapel. There is a type of slender decorated stone pulpit peculiar to Shepton Mallet and the northeast of the county. It may also be seen at Banwell [63b], Brockley, Compton Bishop, Hutton, Locking, Loxton, Wick St. Lawrence, and Worle.[1]

Of the numerous later stone fonts the finest are probably the perfected quatrefoil types at Minehead and Taunton St. Mary. A fine series of figures surrounds the font at Taunton St. James, and at Nettlecombe is the only Somerset example of the Seven Sacraments.

[1] Mrs. D. P. Dobson-Hinton in P 1949.

IV. Smaller Churches and Minor Sculpture

THE LOWER church at Stocklinch, that of St. Mary Magdalene [77], a few miles away from Ile Abbots, is the type of many other little chapels in this district, once dependent on a larger mother church and built to serve an outlying population or the needs of the manor house, as at Ashington [72], Brympton [35b] or Swell. When made of good material these simple buildings without aisle or tower are very pleasing. A chancel, a nave slightly wider, a south porch, and a bell-cot of varying design and size perched on the western gable are their normal components. Some of them have relics of an earlier period: there is a Norman door at Swell and at Chesterblade, a thirteenth-century chancel at Ashington; here the windows are deeply splayed, and have foliated rear-arches and some fine heads on their label stops. The nave windows at Ashington have the wide hollow moulding, inside and out, of the great period, such as we saw at Norton. The church was attractively pewed in the seventeenth century in the manner of the neighbouring church of Mudford. Stripped of its accretions, Brympton is of the same dimensions, with an overgrown bell-cot. It helps to complete the loveliest architectural composition in the county or perhaps in all England. Other churches of the same modest type are at East Lambrook, Chilthorne Domer, Thorne, Curland, and Seavington St. Michael. The curious structure at Lopen, enlarged in 1833, and doubtless many other larger buildings, seem to have developed from this simple plan.

Three churches which are not architecturally typical or important are noteworthy for their situation or their associations. Few are more beautifully placed than Moorlinch, on a terrace of the Polden Hills looking over the wide and flat expanse of Sedgemoor towards Windwhistle, Blackdown, the Brendons, and the Quantocks [64b]. From a higher point in the neighbourhood, on Slocombe, the author has delighted to count some twenty-three towers, but the best view is that with this squat one in the foreground. The rugged architecture of Oare is suited to a very different setting in the far west: it is the church familiar to readers of *Lorna Doone*, and above it stretch the bracken- and heather-covered hills of Exmoor [65]. Northover [64a] was once a suburb of Ilchester. Roger Bacon's friary, the five

57

churches of the town, the gaol, and the rotten borough have successively disappeared, and this little church on the hill surveys the deserted site. When W. W. Wheatley drew this picture, now in the Braikenridge Collection at Taunton, in 1847, he doubtless had the feeling around him of air and space and distance. Yet now, though the building is essentially the same, the little mound on which it stands is overgrown, and the ancient town below has receded still further into the past. There is an atmosphere which changes the character of stone.

The minor sculpture which appears round tower tops and beneath parapets, on corbels, capitals, and label stops, and in other places has been occasionally noticed already. An exhaustive list would be impossible and tedious, but much survives unnoticed, even in churches which are unattractive and heavily restored. Much also passes unobserved because of the interest in larger features. These are a few examples taken almost at random: there is a Trinity and a Virgin and Child in the tower at Brislington and at East Brent, which also has a Coronation; above the chancel arch at Langridge is an impressive statue of the Madonna and Child, which may date from the twelfth century; at Hatch Beauchamp there is a Resurrection; at Hatch Beauchamp again, and also at Watchet and Flax Bourton, there is a George or Michael and the Dragon; at Flax Bourton this is Norman work. There are some very fine heads and beasts of the best period of early Gothic carving (*c.* 1220) round some stranded capitals in the reduced choir of Queen Charlton. Two little heads in the chancels of Orchardleigh and Portishead in all probability supported the Lenten veil. We may mention also: three praying figures on the tower of Closworth; a mysterious group on the east gable at Ashington; a charming squirrel and a dog on a capital at Preston Plucknett; a fox chasing a goose round a column in the nave arcade at Lydeard St. Lawrence; the arms of St. Joseph, adopted by Abbot Selwood, at Meare; a tooth being extracted at Monksilver; an extremely fine series of beasts and angels on the interior label stops in the windows at Thornfalcon; the thirteenth-century anti-clerical roof corbels at Hemington,[1] a lute player, a woman telling her beads, devils, and heads of an elephant, a rhinoceros, and a toad, on the tower at Camerton; superb angels and evangelistic symbols, whose outspread wings embrace almost the whole tower top, at Bicknoller; two fantastic satyric figures under the tower arch at Beer Crocombe. These, with gargoyles and corbel heads innumerable are a sure indication of the freedom left to the medieval carver and a tribute to his skill and fantasy.

---

[1] P 1911, p. 64. See also *N & Q*, xxiii, 41, *Medieval Portrait Heads* by A. W. Vivian-Neal: a thirteenth-century head of a pope at the north door at Bridgwater is there reproduced.

V. Glass

THE FRAGMENTS of old glass which remain forgotten in the tracery lights of so many of our windows are the relics of a lost glory, of which Protestantism and neglect have robbed us. The eager and scholarly researches of Dr. Woodforde, who comes of the family of another Somerset cleric whose diaries have made a different contribution to our knowledge, have put new light into these little patches of colour, even in the most unpromising places.[1] He finds over a hundred and fifty churches which still contain them: they are a wonderful mine for iconography and for local history, and he has richly exploited it. To give but one example: most visitors to the moorland church of Mark will have admired its tower, its proportions, and the big figures of the Evangelists imported from Flanders, but they are unlikely to have noticed, under the fine roof in the north aisle, among heads of the apostles and emblems of the Passion, a coat of arms containing three guns and a female figure below holding a spray of flowers. The guns are the arms of John Gunthorpe, Dean of Wells, a scholar, book collector, and diplomat, one of the bearers of the Renaissance to England; the flowers recall the exquisite legend of St. Dorothy. As will be expected, this glass mostly comes from our golden age. Except in the cathedral, there are few pieces before the fifteenth century. A few windows survive on a bigger scale, and the most important of these I will now enumerate.

(1) A window at Alford, re-arranged in 1935, makes a very pleasing effect in that very pretty little church. (2) Banwell. There is a small scene from the life of St. Nicholas, patron of children, who delivers a child from a boiling cauldron; also several others of Netherland origin from Tobit and the Bible. (3) East Brent. (a) A north window, late fifteenth century, probably the gift of Abbot Selwood, representing St. James, St. John, and St. John the Baptist. (b) A Passion window with some nine scenes at the east end of the same north aisle. Most of the glass here dates from about 1850 but it bears such strong traces of medieval design, and the colour is so good for that date, that it was almost certainly copied from one which was there before; in the same way, but with much less happy effect, Winchester College provided itself with a new set of windows in 1821. At East Brent it has so far been impossible to discover what Victorian firm did the work,

---

[1] Christopher Woodforde, *Stained Glass in Somerset*, 1946.

but it seems to me that it was done by the firm that restored the east window at Drayton Beauchamp in Buckinghamshire at about the same time. (4) Farleigh Hungerford. A knight in armour, perhaps Sir Thomas Hungerford, who built Wellow, and died in 1398. Also much seventeenth- and eighteenth-century foreign glass in small panels. (5) Langport. In the east window there are ten large figures and many smaller ones, along with the arms of John Heron, Portreeve, d. 1499, and Amias Poulett, his executor. These were happily collected together here from various parts of the church in 1867. Here, too, in red and blue robes, is the figure of St. Joseph of Arimathea, bearing with him to Glastonbury the two cruets with the Blood and Sweat of Our Lord. (6) Orchardleigh. Six smaller windows with figures of apostles and others, including a very beautiful Trinity, made at different dates between 1430 and 1520, and perhaps by a small firm in Bath or Bristol, for the style is not that which is generally used by the Somerset school. (7) St. Catherine's, near Bath, has an east window with the three figures of the rood, and St. Peter, much restored, and replaced a hundred years ago. These are accompanied by a request for prayer for John Cantelow, Prior of Bath, who built the chancel in 1490. (8) Trull. In the chancel three martial figures, St. Michael, St. Margaret, and St. George demolish dragons; the two male saints are in the armour of the late fifteenth century. (9) Winscombe contains more old glass than any other church in the county. There is a fine rood group along with St. Anthony and donors. There is also a window with an inscription commemorating Peter Carslegh, vicar, who died in 1534—a Devonshire man of substance and influence, Canon of Wells and one of the theologians who promoted Henry VIII's divorce. In the last years of his life he prayed for Queen Catherine instead of Queen Anne in Wells Cathedral, on which his wretched Bishop saw fit to delate him to Cromwell, excusing him however on the ground that he was an old man and 'the word scapyd hym unwars ex lapsu lingue'.[1] The glass has three saints of his name, Peter the Apostle, Peter the Deacon, Peter the Exorcist; its late date is attested by the Renaissance cherubs and cornucopia in its heads. (10) Cheddar has some angels and good heraldic glass, with arms of the local families of Cheddar, Rodney, Pyne, Newton, and Roe, c. 1470–80. Dr. Woodforde is of the opinion that most of these windows are of local manufacture and design. Some of them, including Langport, contain in their backgrounds what he has called the Somerset quarry, a fleur-de-lis, of various designs, which is almost confined to the county.

[1] State Papers of Henry VIII. I. 427.

VI. Medieval Monuments

THE LATE Dr. A. C. Fryer has described with patient skill and sympathy the medieval monuments of the county.[1] On stylistic and geological grounds he has established the chief schools of imagers who worked here. There were at first three: those of Wells, Bristol, and Ilchester. The school of Wells used the local Doulting stone and first practised their craft in the greatest of medieval training grounds, the building of a great cathedral. When that cathedral was Wells in the thirteenth century, it will easily be understood that they received some inspiration. On the completion of their chief task there, on the great west façade, it is probable that they moved on to reinforce the masons of Bristol. The opportunities afforded by the wealth, population, and communications of the third city of England[2] soon gave this school, which drew on the quarries of Dundry, local pre-eminence. They flourished until the seventeenth century, but their greatest achievements were in the third quarter of the fifteenth. The most splendid tombs in our churches are Bristol work of that time. The third native school, which we find at work in the thirteenth and fourteenth centuries, is that of Ilchester or its neighbourhood, which used the stone of Ham Hill and which may also have originated at Wells. To these three native schools was added, at the beginning of the fourteenth century, that of Bath, which had a good stone at its doors and was still turning out effigies in the sixteenth century.

In addition to these four Somerset stones, we find, as in other parts of England, the work of the Purbeck marblers from Dorset and also that of the Exeter school which used the soft white stone of Beer. The former lost their market by about 1280, and the Exeter monuments are not very numerous here. The four local schools were the chief source of supply for their own districts, and they held their own against the Derbyshire alabaster which was so widely used throughout the Midlands after the middle of the fourteenth century. In Somerset only nine effigies, four of them in Wells Cathedral, were made of this rich and beautiful material before the Reformation. For a century afterwards, with improved communications, it was the chief material for tombs throughout the whole country. It appears

[1] In P 1915-30.
[2] After York, H. E. Darby, *Historical Geography of England before 1800*, 1936.

61

that alabaster from Blue Anchor was not used in the Middle Ages.[1] In the mid-seventeenth century the Derbyshire veins deteriorated and foreign marbles took their place.

The first effigies in Wells Cathedral were made about 1200, the façade by Bishop Jocelin between 1206 and 1242, and the first effigy in the county outside, like the first Somerset tower, may be at Shepton Mallet, where there is a figure in Doulting stone of an unknown knight (about 1240), showing the ripple folds of the sculpture of Wells. From 1260 to 1270 date some effigies of the de Urtiaco family, under arched recesses at Curry Rivel, and of the Raleighs at Nettlecombe. The two de Gyverney knights and their ladies still rest under the effigies made for them in their chapel at Limington (c. 1330.[2]) All these are in Ham Hill stone and of the chain mail period, and the beauty of their surroundings and material increase their pathetic appeal. Of more intrinsic interest, and in better preservation, is the tomb of Sir John de Domer at Pendomer (1325) [66]. The figure lies under a cinquefoil-headed arch with angel cusps, above which is a battlemented cornice, supported by two rough peasant caryatids. The cornice still holds iron spikes on which candles were lit on Sir John's obit. Later in the fourteenth century, but in Bath stone and in exquisite but very different settings, are the figures of Sir Matthew and Lady Stawell at Cothelstone on the western slope of Quantock, and of a lady who may be Eleanor de Beauchamp, wife of Richard Pyke, at Moorlinch. The Stawells and the Pykes were once great families in Somerset. Of the numerous ecclesiastics of the period the most striking is at Brympton (c. 1420), but he owes his fine features to a skilful Victorian artist.[3] The numerous effigies in Wells Cathedral, including Bishop William de Marchia (1302) and the unknown ecclesiastic in the chapel of St. Calixtus with the exquisite alabaster reliefs, fall outside the scope of this work. Two effigies in oak survive in the county: one, at Chew Magna, reclines in a hideous posture and was restored some seventy years ago to an unhealthy state of coloured animation: the other still moulders, nameless, in the last stages of decay in a tower chamber at Midsomer Norton.

The golden age of our churches is reflected in its monuments, and if they are not so numerous nor continued to so late a date as our finest achievements in architecture, yet there is a select company which attains almost the highest excellence. Sir Thomas Hungerford, first titular Speaker of the Commons and the traditional builder of the church at Wellow (d. 1398) and his wife (d. 1412) have a splendid tomb with shields, weepers, grille, and traces of colour, in the castle chapel of Farleigh Hungerford, made in

[1] See below, p. 74.
[2] See above, p. 21.
[3] The late John Batten related that this was a Mr. Carew: he deserves commemoration.

Bath stone. The great tombs of this period are adorned with canopies, and occupy a prominent position in the church, as at Henstridge or Spaxton between the chancel and the aisles. Both of these came from the Wells workshops, although they are at opposite ends of the county, and date about 1460. The Carent tomb at Henstridge has much of its original colour. A more famous and ambitious monument is at Porlock, to Lord and Lady Harington. Lord Harington was knighted in the French wars by Henry V and died young in 1418; in his will, dated 1417, he expressed the desire to found a chantry, but this was not carried out until after his widow's death, no less than fifty-six years later. The figures are in alabaster, c. 1460, but the architectural work in the light and beautiful canopy, which remains from the chantry chapel, was made in Bristol of Dundry stone about 1474.

The culmination of all this work is to be found in St. Mary Redcliffe, Bristol (no longer to be counted a Somerset Church), Long Ashton and Yatton, in five splendid monuments. At St. Mary Redcliffe are the two life-like effigies of William Canynges, one of the builders of the church, first as Lord Mayor, and then as Priest and Dean of the College which he founded at Westbury-on-Trym (c. 1490). Thirty years separate these two effigies. The first, in Dundry stone, was made in his lifetime after his wife's death; the second, in alabaster, is a memorial erected sixteen years after his own death in 1474. In the same church is the even grander tomb of Sir Thomas and Lady Mede, in stone, 1475. The design of this tomb and of the very similar and contemporary one at Long Ashton to Sir Richard Choke and his wife have all the surety and perfection which an artistic tradition attains in its classical stage [68b]. Five ogee arches growing into heavily crocketed finials form a horizontal canopy over the two figures at Long Ashton. Between them, four charming angel busts spread their up-turned wings along the shafts of pinnacles set in diagonal section and re-peating the motifs of the finials alongside. These are set against a back-ground of slender trefoil-headed panels for which the note is sounded on the lower face of the tomb as well. To the sides the pinnacle motif is taken up in tall enclosing clusters. On the wall surface behind, two angels in relief with long wings hold up a coat of arms and scrolls with prayers. The stage where every ornament falls into its place with almost mechanical precision is indeed a far cry from Sir John de Domer's rough peasants.

Sir Richard Choke was a judge. A yet more eminent lawyer was Sir Richard Newton, Lord Chief Justice of the Court of Common Pleas, whose table-tomb at Yatton was made in alabaster about 1470 [68a]. His features also are too fine and individual to be other than a portrait; in niches all round the monument are shield-bearing angels in the best alabaster tradition. To the east of this, Sir Richard's son, Sir John Newton, who died

63

in 1487, made at the same time and during his lifetime the most magnificent of all Somerset tombs for himself and his wife. The design is more elaborate and perhaps not so satisfactory as those other two contemporary stone monuments which we have just examined. The open quatrefoil, heavily cusped and with feathered centres, is the chief decorative motif. A relief of the Annunciation has survived at the back of the recess. The arch-angelic wings have the distinct quills and feathers characteristic of the south-west, but the panels are influenced by the alabaster men, perhaps those same men whom Sir John employed to do the tomb of his father. All this lies in the chapel which he and his wife constructed for the church in which they, like the other people of Yatton, took so great a pride. Other good work of this time and school may be seen at Backwell and Rodney Stoke. It is strange that no notable monuments of the early sixteenth century in the great tradition are to be found in our churches. Yet they abound in the west of England. That at Wraxall to Lady Anne Howard and her husband Sir Edmund Gorges, is already of a different character, strongly Renaissance in type, although Dr. Fryer had reason to think it was made as early as 1495, shortly after her death.

VII. Brasses

THERE ARE few medieval brasses of importance in Somerset, and the art has not for us the interest which local material and style gives to our effigies; they were largely a London product, and though latterly they were cut and engraved in a few other counties, the material was the same, and foreign, and the style showed only minor differences.[1] There are, however, three good examples in our churches, two of which are of the first rank and in excellent preservation. The third, that of Thomas Chedder (1443), son of a Bristol mayor, in the church of his name, has lost its inscription and shields and is the exact counterpart of others at Ewelme in Oxfordshire, Preston in Kent, and at Westminster Abbey. The other two are those of Sir William and Lady Wadham at Ilminster, and of Sir Giles and Lady Daubeney at South Petherton. Sir William Wadham, the traditional builder of the north transept at Ilminster, who died in 1452, built a noble altar tomb for himself and his mother during his own lifetime. This long afterwards inspired the splendid monument, in the same place and style, of his descendant Nicholas Wadham, who died in 1618. There is no finer post-Reformation brass in England than that of the founder of Wadham College.[2] The illustration shows the morning sunlight on the fine tomb which Sir Giles Daubeney put up to himself and his first wife during his lifetime (in about 1430) in the south transept at South Petherton [67]. On the floor alongside is a separate brass to his second wife, who died in 1442. Sir Giles is seen in armour of the best period, accompanied by canopies, shields, and inscriptions. His wife has a horned head-dress, slender waist, jewels, and long flowing mantle. Sir Giles lived at Barrington near by and was Sheriff of Somerset, Dorset, Buckinghamshire and Bedfordshire, where his other estates lay. The effigies stand on a rich pedestal of Ham Hill stone, adorned with elaborate quatrefoils, shields, and angels.

The other medieval brasses in the county are smaller and more ordinary work. It will suffice to mention two at Beckington which Mr. Connor describes and illustrates.[3] The little figure of John Seyntmaur is in armour

[1] For this section I am chiefly indebted to the work already mentioned, of Mr. A. B. Connor, in P 1931 ff.

[2] That to his brother-in-law, John Wyndham, at St. Decuman's, which was probably made after 1596, is however evidently by the same hand and of almost equal merit. P 1931, p. 87. Also see Dr. Eeles's description of St. Decuman's, Cox and Sons, Williton, 1932.

[3] P 1932.

at its most fantastic development (*c.* 1485): his wife has a close-fitting gown, delicate waist, and butterfly head-dress. If they ever appeared thus together they would have been a striking pair. In strong contrast are the demure and contemporary figures of John Compton and his wife in long, full, furred gown and cuffs (1505). Above their heads two little angels are given the incongruous task of holding beer barrels with his rebus (the letters '*J. cum*' on a tun). His will is extant[1] and contains many pious and sensible benefactions, some of which are typical of the 'clothmen' to whom our great churches are largely due. There is the usual small fee to the church of Wells, 3*s.* 4*d.*; there is £20 to his parish church, part of which is to be spent on two silver gilt candelabra; a further £20 to be distributed among seventeen other parish churches at the discretion of his executors. Bath Abbey and the two Carthusian houses of Witham and Hinton also receive gifts, and the four orders of Friars in Bristol are given money to sing trentals for the souls of himself and his parents. He also leaves money for the repair of roads and streets and to help the marriage of sixteen poor girls.

[1] S.R.S., xix, pp. 47, 114.

VIII. The Seventeenth Century

THE SIXTEENTH century, which began so gloriously for our churches, was in its latter half an age of sorrow, decay, and destruction. The Church was pillaged, her clergy reduced and impoverished, her people no longer delighted to adorn her. From her spoils, from her very stone, the new rich built their mansions; the common people copied this example and ceased their offerings. Their hopes of the hereafter were no longer thus fortified. The roods, whose recent cult had helped to raise the clerestories and the roofs, were shattered along with the screen balconies and the coloured glass. Whitewash or texts replaced St. Christopher, the Doom, and the Saints on the walls. Many more of the structures themselves would have gone the same way if a revival of church principles had not been fostered by the first two Stuart kings. Laud, the most active figure in this movement, was Bishop of Bath and Wells from 1626 to 1628, and the work was vigorously pursued by his disciple William Piers (1632–70), under whom no less than a hundred and fifty Somerset altars were restored to the east end in a single year (1634). His work was undone and he was savagely persecuted by the Puritans, but he lived to see their final discomfiture.

Besides many other traces, three complete little churches of the Counter-Reformation survive in Somerset, those of Low Ham, Wyke Champflower and Rodden. Rodden, which was built in 1640, is relatively uninteresting. Low Ham [70a] appears at first sight ordinary Somerset Perpendicular, but it was begun by Sir Edward Hext, who died in 1623, and completed, after damage in the wars, by his grandson George Stawell between 1660 and 1690. It is one of the most perfect examples in England of the late persistence of the Gothic tradition. It is built of the local lias, and has on a small scale all the members of the fifteenth-century church: western tower, chancel, aisles, arcade, clerestory, and screen. It might be High Ham's late child, with few of its finer graces but much of its charm. Externally its members are not well-connected, and its tracery will not bear close inspection. The later work includes the pulpit, the finely carved royal arms, the altar frontal, still in use, which falls in folds at the corners, the glass of the east window[1] and the screen. The memory of the elaborate funeral of Sir John Stawell in 1662 and its procession to his burial-place at Cothelstone,

[1] Described and illustrated by Dr. Woodforde, p. 237.

67

some twenty miles away to the west is ever present.[1] Above a pretty row of winged cherub heads on the screen runs the appropriate text: 'My sonne, feare God and the Kinge and meddle not with them that are given to change' (*Proverbs*, xxiv, 21) [71]. The church stands in melancholy isolation in the middle of a field, the only relic but for a few walls and terraces of a great house which the second Lord Stawell planned but had not the funds to complete.

Under a similar influence Henry Southworth built the church at Wyke Champflower [74a] near Bruton, as an annexe to his house, in 1624. It has a western turret and flat-headed Tudor windows; there is a rich stone pulpit, pews and rails of the period, and a great display of heraldry in the low, coved, and plastered roof. Above the sanctuary rails there is a large tympanum but no screen below it. In its centre facing west are the royal arms, and on either side those of the sees of Canterbury and of Bath and Wells, impaling those of Abbot and Lake, their occupants in 1624.[2]

Three wagon roofs received embellishments in the Laudian revival; Axbridge [74b] in 1636, East Brent [75] in 1637 (both are dated), and Muchelney [73] perhaps rather earlier. Axbridge and East Brent have patterns in plaster, Muchelney is painted. East Brent is a freer and rougher version of the formal and finished design of Axbridge: its cusps are more Gothic, its writing, as it were, more cursive: the plaster worker who arranged his pattern so precisely at Axbridge and divided it into neat compartments seems to have left his ruler behind him when he crossed the flats next year to East Brent, and to have trusted to his eye; yet the pattern, if carefully examined, will be found to be essentially the same. The effect at Brent when the brown paint flakes off and leaves a golden tone is very happy: this was repainted some thirty years ago. The painting at Muchelney has about it something of the Continental baroque and has reminded a Czech friend of the author of her native land. Each panel holds an angel in feathered tights standing securely on very solid clouds and holding scrolls with texts and invitations to 'come up hither'. Something similar may be seen at Bromfield in Shropshire, where the chancel roof was painted in 1658.[3]

East Brent contains also a gallery (1635), a pulpit (1634) and pewter candlesticks of the same time. All these Laudian features blend happily, as they always do with late Perpendicular work. The gallery here, like that of Rodney Stoke, is an interesting survival of pre-Reformation practice.

---

[1] *v.* Col. G. D. Stawell, *A Quantock Family*, Barnicott and Pearce, 1910, p. 406; Preb. D. M. Ross in the *Proceedings* of the Bath Branch of the S.A.S., 1941, p. 142; the present author in the *Geographical Magazine*, Apr. and Nov. 1940.

[2] *N. & Q.*, vi, 101.

[3] *Country Life*, 9 September 1949.

The carpenter's bill survives for work done in 1824 at a total cost of £185. 11s. This includes the removal of the gallery to the west end where it now stands, the making of its present supporting pillars, of a Gothic screen between the church and chancel where the present gallery formerly stood, and of a partition above it. It is not clear from this whether the medieval screen survived until then to support the Caroline gallery. No traces of it or of the 1824 Gothic survived the erection of the present chancel in 1845.[1] Better known is the stupendous display of woodwork in the rich clothiers' town of Croscombe, dated 1616, which again mingles easily with rich carving of the great period [76]. The chancel roof here was put up in 1664, which date it bears; it is of the traditional tie-beam construction.

At Kittisford the north chapel with a wooden arcade was built in the un-promising year 1659 in a style of its own which yet shows Gothic influ-ences.[2] A Tudor window of three lights with cinquefoil heads in the south aisle at Allerton bears the date 1638. The Rodney chapel at Rodney Stoke is one of the most moving memorials of its age. Sir Edward Rodney, the last of his line, whose family monuments are there, also built other work in the church, including a fine screen with open balustrade above, a thing very rare at that time (1625).

Two large towers in north Somerset were erected in the seventeenth century. The former central tower[3] at Keynsham fell in 1632, and follow-ing the procedure of two hundred years earlier a new and much bigger one was then erected at the west. This took two hundred years to build and exhibits in its three stages the gradual decline of the Gothic feeling. Yet it is not without dignity and merit. The screen now placed in front of the organ in the chancel and, it would seem, the roof of the south aisle also date from the Laudian revival. The tower of Midsomer Norton, dated 1674 and bearing a statue of Charles II, is also a massive example of seventeenth-century Gothic.

The age usually called Jacobean has, however, left much wider traces behind it in the furniture than in the structure of our churches. Jacobean pulpits are almost as numerous as Norman fonts, and it would be as tedious to enumerate them. A particularly fine example is at St. Cuthbert's Wells (1636). The finest array of seating of the period is at Mudford, and the style is copied at Ashington, the next village [72]. Similar work may be

[1] As this matter is frequently misunderstood, these details from the carpenter's bill of 1824 may be of interest. 'Removing gallery to west end . . . equal to labour of five men, 45 days each at 3/-, £33. 15.' This included 'putting up the partition at the back of the Gallery and over where the old Gallery stood'. 'A Gothic Screen between the Church and Chancel' measuring 169 feet at 3s. 6d. cost some £29. 'Altering and framing part of the front of the Gallery and making framing to match with carved rails, panels etc.' cost 15s.

[2] P 1912, p. 64.

[3] Its actual position was apparently at the east end of the north aisle.

seen at Great Elm and elsewhere. The neighbouring churches of Thurloxton (1634), Stoke St. Gregory, and North Newton have pulpits with
figures of the Virtues, etc., upon them. North Newton has the five wise
and the five foolish virgins on the vestry door, and some carvings at Stoke
may also be relics of the same subject. The altar at Somerton has small
biblical scenes round its bulbous legs. At Bridgwater the magnificent
screen which now dignifies the mayoral pew was designed to cross the
nave.

IX. Seventeenth-Century Monuments

THANKS IN large measure to the persistent efforts of Mrs. Esdaile, the monuments of the Renaissance in English churches have recovered from the neglect and contempt of the last century, but they are not represented in Somerset by many examples of outstanding merit. Much the most imposing series of family monuments is that of the Pouletts at Hinton St. George. To the east of the carpeted and upholstered family pew is a square room which contains the chief of these. There are many others in the body of the church of a later date, but none on their scale. Sir Hugh Poulett, who died in 1573, erected in his lifetime the pair of tombs to himself and his father [69], Sir Amias I, who was knighted for his part in the defeat of Lambert Simnel at Newark in 1487, and died in 1538. This fierce and virile work was done in Beer stone at Exeter. In it the Gothic quatrefoil and something like the classical acanthus leaf and Renaissance mask are strangely mingled, and dominated by the three silver swords of the Pouletts. Of much more accomplished design is the monument of Amias II (d. 1588), the guardian of Mary Queen of Scots, who to his everlasting credit refused Elizabeth's request quietly to put away his inconvenient captive, with the words 'God forbid that I should make such a shipwreck of my conscience'. The monument stood until 1728 in St. Martin-in-the-Fields, and it bears inscriptions not only in Latin and English (one composed by 'E.R.'— Elizabeth?) but also in French to 'ce preux chevalier, ce Renomme Seigneur', which is surely the last time that this language was used in our epigraphy. The workmanship bears all the marks of the Southwark school, and is far superior to anything of the same period in the county. Amias's son, Sir Anthony, who died in 1600, lies under a handsome Renaissance monument of uncoloured Bath stone whose coved canopy, obelisks, and massive achievement are supported by finely carved Corinthian columns. Yet in the shape of the arch and the postures of the kneeling children around the base the Gothic influence is not quite dead. The fifth and last in this chapel is a fantastic accumulation of coloured stucco made, in Mrs. Esdaile's opinion, at Bristol after the Restoration for John, 1st Lord Poulett [81], who died in 1649. This, as Mr. Sacheverell Sitwell has remarked, is redolent of Spain or Sicily where perhaps some of the Pouletts spent their exile. A full-skirted angel, a swag of bright flowers, a tasselled knotted curtain, two hairy

71

woodmen, skulls, lions, torches, two crown-bearing cherubs, and tapering fluted columns are all disposed about the empty sarcophagus.

Rodney Stoke, at the foot of Mendip, has, after St. Decuman's, the only series comparable with that at Hinton St. George. A canopy of knotted curtains, angels, and cherubs, perhaps of Bristol work, overhangs the busts of Sir Edward Rodney and his wife, who gave all for their king and, having lost their only son, knew they were the last of their line [80]. His family had been leaders in the county for over three hundred and fifty years: 'it is rather', he wrote,[1] 'a blessing to have lasted so long than a punishment to end at last'. He died without seeing the Restoration, in 1657. His son George in his shroud half emerges from his stone tomb at the trump of the little angel in the clouds above. A similar work at Steane in Northamptonshire is known to be by the brothers Christmas. The third tomb contains the beautiful recumbent figure of Anne Rodney, who died in 1630, in alabaster under a slender arch dotted on the underside with little clouds. Its sarcophagus resembles the elder Sir John Stawell's tomb at Cothelstone which Mrs. Esdaile attributes to Epiphanius Evesham.[2]

There are three wall monuments in Curry Mallet, a large one to John Pyne and his wife, a charming one to an unknown girl, and another to the parson, in beard and ruff, and holding the Bible, all in alabaster. Of the other bigger monuments those to Robert and Marmaduke Jennings, 1630, with its fine iron grill and mysterious little padlocked chest, at Curry Rivel [78],[3] to Sir Nicholas Halswell (1633), at Goathurst [79], and to Edward Winter (1673) at Clapton-in-Gordano are perhaps the most interesting, if not the most recognized.

Before relegating the remaining effigies to a footnote in order to preserve the scale of this book, two works in bronze must be mentioned which attain a perfection far higher than that of any other Somerset monument of their time. The gilt bronze bust at Bruton of young Mr. William Godolphin [82], who died in 1636, has been tentatively attributed by Mr. Geoffrey Webb to Hubert le Sueur, who would have no reason to be ashamed of it.[4] In a dark corner of the noble church of St. Decuman's, Watchet, are the embossed shield, mantling, and half-figures of Sir John and Joan Wyndham [83]. Mr. R. H. d'Elboux has identified the great gravestone in which these are set as that which was ordered from Nicholas Stone in 1634, in Sir John's lifetime, after his wife's death in the preceding year. Yet the

[1] In a memoir, a copy of which is kept in the vicarage.
[2] The present author in the *Geographical Magazine*, May and November 1940.
[3] Curry Rivel has a fine series of monuments ranging from the thirteenth century to the little tablet put up 'by me Hester Countess of Chatham' [widow of the Great Commoner, whose estate of Burton Pynsent is in the parish] 'to a most excellent worthy servant who made me feel the gratitude she deserved from me'.
[4] Illustration in P 1934, and *Burlington Magazine*, lii, p. 88.

account in Stone's notebooks, which is otherwise very detailed, makes no mention of the brass plates which are the chief feature of the monument, and to whose superlative grace and workmanship it would be good to attach a name.[1]

Finally, Mr. Connor has shown how beautiful are the lettering and engraving of many of the numerous brass plates and indeed, we may add, of the ledger stones to humbler people at this time. There are also an unusual number of what we may call picture brasses, among these we may mention those of Humphrey Willis of Wells, the Strode brass at Shepton Mallet, and the memorials of the Biss family at Croscombe and Batcombe. Two very pleasing brasses at Wedmore commemorate two proud soldiers, father and son, Thomas and George Hodges, the one by an exquisite inscription, the other by his martial figure in jackboots, spurs, sword, and pike. Their dates are 1600 and 1634 respectively.

Besides those mentioned already, the following churches have monuments with effigies of dates between 1540 and 1600—a period whose style is essentially the same as that of the seventeenth century:

Bruton	Sir Maurice Berkeley, 1581	*(stone)*
Chew Magna	Edmund Baber, 1571	*(stone)*
Dunster	Thomas Luttrell, 1570	*(alabaster)*
East Harptree	Sir John Newton, 1568	*(stone)*
Heathfield	Arthur Hadley, *c.* 1595	*(stone)*
Kenn	Sir Christopher Kenn, 1593	
Keynsham	Sir Henry Brydges, 1587	*(stone)*
Montacute	Thomas Phelips, 1588	*(stone)*
Pitminster	Humphrey Colles, 1570	*(stone)*
Wells, St. Cuthbert's	Henry Clarke, 1587	*(stone)*

And without effigies there are the following of some importance:

Charlton Adam	Thomas Basket, 1572	*(stone)*
White Lackington	George Speke, *c.* 1580	*(stone)*

The following have seventeenth-century effigies:

Axbridge	William and Anne Prowse, 1670	*(stone)*
Barrow Gurney	Francis James, 1616	*(stone)*
Bickenhall	Rachel Portman, 1632	*(alabaster)*
Bishop's Hull	George Farwell, 1609	*(alabaster)*
Bridgwater	Francis Kingsmill, 1620	*(alabaster)*
South Brent	John Somerset, 1664	*(stone)*
Butleigh	Fragments, *c.* 1610	*(stone)*
Chard	William Brewer, 1618	*(alabaster)*

[1] P 1947. Walpole Society, vol. vii, p. 100.

Churchill	John Latch (*stone*)
Claverton	Sir William Bassett, 1613 (*alabaster*)
West Coker	Grace and Elizabeth Portman, *c.* 1640 (*stone*)
Cothelstone	Sir John Stawell, 1603 (*alabaster*)
Low Ham	Sir Edward Hext, 1624 (*stone*)
South Petherton	Henry Compton, 1603 (*stone*)
South Petherton	William Ayshe, 1657 (*stone*)
Pitminster	John Colles, 1607 (*alabaster*)
Pitminster	John Colles, 1627 (*alabaster*)
Taunton	Robert Gray, 1635 (*alabaster*)
Watchet	Henry and George Wyndham, 1624 (*alabaster*)
Wellington	Chief Justice Popham, 1607 (*alabaster*)
Wiveliscombe	Humphrey Windham, 1622 (*alabaster*)

And without effigy:

Brympton	John Sydenham, 1626 (*stone*)

It may be of interest to note that of the monuments before 1600 only two, and those of the most important families, Poulett and Luttrell, are in alabaster. In the seventeenth century more than twelve are in this material, including those of William Brewer 'phisitian'. By this time it became a cheaper material, and perhaps for that reason the supplies became exhausted. There is an outcrop of alabaster on the coast near Blue Anchor, and there is evidence to show that this was largely drawn upon in the seventeenth century.[1] It is therefore probable that several of the other monuments here mentioned came from Somerset rather than Derbyshire quarries. More evidence of its quarrying and use, perhaps outside the county, would be of interest. For the most part however these monuments no longer betray local characteristics, but there is one exception. It would seem that the stone monuments of Edward Rodney, 1657, John Somerset, 1664, and William Prowse, 1670, are by the same man; moreover they are in the same area.[2]

[1] In 1633 Thomas Gerard wrote 'A Particular Description of Somerset'. Speaking of 'Mynhead', he says 'at this place in our tyme a Duch man hath found out mynes of excellent Alabaster which they use much for Tombes and Chimneypeeces'. S.R.S., xv, 12. The font at Williton is made of it.

[2] Dr. Eeles in P 1945, p. 37.

X. The Eighteenth Century

THERE REMAIN now in our churches fewer traces of the eighteenth century than of its predecessor. Babington (1750) is the best example of a building wholly of this period, neat, compact, and assured, both within and without [84]; its sanctuary fittings are those of an elegant drawing-room. Less happy except for good plaster work in the ceiling is the centrally planned little structure at Berkley (1751) near Frome, standing up against its manor house. Two churches built in noblemen's parks on the eastern side of the county date from the end of the century, Redlynch and Marston Bigot, built respectively for the Earls of Ilchester and Cork: the latter is filled with most interesting foreign glass. Foxcote and Woolley (1761) are two others wholly built in the classical style, under the influence of Bath. They are small, sensible, and unpretentious, and with the passage of years have acquired a certain attraction. This was not felt by the squires and clergy of the nineteenth century; filled with holy zeal they destroyed the furnishings and many of the structures and monuments of an age which they disliked. They established the principle, which is still in the bones of most Englishmen, that church architecture must be medieval. One forgotten little church in the Mendip country, however, though structurally medieval of various dates, has been left intact in its eighteenth-century condition. As such Cameley must be among the best period pieces in England [85]. A western gallery was erected in 1711, a southern one, 'for the free use of the inhabitants', in 1819; they are approached by an external staircase. A low Norman arch, heavily whitewashed, separates the chancel from the nave and supports a large tablet with the Commandments and the Lord's Prayer; they are faced by a Norman font and a big painted royal arms under the tower arch; between them a tall rickety stove pipe ascends to the roof. Around it are disposed at haphazard a two-decker Jacobean pulpit and box pews and low pews of both centuries. There is more Hanoverian woodwork in the sanctuary, and high up in the galleries on both sides of the tower arch are rows of hat-pegs for the inhabitants. A tablet below the Commandments boasts the high descent through both his parents of Cadwallader Jones (1692), and on the north side and on the floor are several nobly carved stones to members of the Mogg family.

Other churches which to a less extent retain their unrestored features and

75

the appearance common in the eighteenth century are Catcott, Pawlett, and Sutton Mallet in the Polden country, Holcombe and Emborrow in the Mendips, Stawley beyond Milverton, and the choir of Bruton. This last was built in 1745 by William Lord Berkeley to replace the chancel of the fourteenth-century church, of which the other relic is the little north tower.[1] The late Perpendicular reconstruction which, as we have seen, built the nave and west tower, and would presumably have destroyed these, was never completed. There are also several tower tops restored in eighteenth-century style, of which the most marked is Priston, which blends with Norman work of the twelfth and nineteenth centuries. At East Woodlands there is a neat tower and spire of 1712–14, when the parish was first constituted. The eighteenth century is also proclaimed by the massive spikes above the tower angles at Marksbury and the little squat ones at North Stoke and at Hinton Charterhouse. The last relic of the great fifteenth-century tradition may be the delicate open-work screen made at Crowcombe in 1729. The earliest neo-Gothic in the county, on the other hand, is the interesting tower of Paulton, dated 1757,[2] and here illustrated [86], which is much superior to the Gothic work in the nave of 1839.

It is a strange thing that with the exception of the crude half-figure of Roger Soudon, vicar of Easton-in-Gordano (1703), a poor bust at Yeovil, and a good one to Sir John Tynte at Goathurst (1742), no eighteenth-century effigies or busts survive in Somerset churches. The most imposing work of the period is at Newton St. Loe, where there is a fine monument in marble but no statue to Joseph Langton (1739) and his family. A large space is railed off at the west end of the south aisle where the font might be expected. On the west wall two detached Corinthian columns support an arch surmounted by urns and cherubs and frame a long Latin inscription with arms and two cherub heads below. The workmanship is of the first order, perhaps by Thomas Green of Camberwell. Otherwise the age of classical taste has left us only minor but numerous wall tablets, some of admirable design and lettering but few of local significance.

---

[1] The architect and builder of the chancel at Bruton was Nathaniel Ireson of Wincanton. H. St. George Gray in P 1941, and *Country Life*, 22 April, 1939.

[2] The faculty dates from 1756, which should prove that the emblem on the tower, which is in this form $1\frac{7}{7}5$, should be read as 1757, and not 1775. The faculty is in the Diocesan Registry at Wells.

XI. The Nineteenth Century

THERE IS good material in Somerset for the study of the medieval revival in architecture during the last century in the first two of its three chief phases. These were: (1) The church building epoch inspired by the Evangelical revival, the fear of revolution, and the Parliamentary grants after the Napoleonic wars. (2) The mid-Victorian era inspired by the Oxford movement, the great era of restoration. (3) The era of repentance, correctness and scholarship since.

(1) In this phase the style usually adopted was a barer development of Strawberry Hill Gothic, but some interesting experiments in Romanesque were also attempted. We can discover now the names of most of the architects.[1] Thus the simple nave of Godney on its low platform above the Brue Levels and the costlier church of Cleeve near Yatton with its triple sanctuary arch were built by G. P. Manners of Bath in 1839 and 1840 respectively. The ambitious building in a Continental Romanesque at Farrington Gurney was designed by John Pinch in 1843. The interior has the frigid dignity of some German work of the period but is by no means without merits. Many of these churches were severely utilitarian and built as cheaply as possible. In these the lancet style was favoured as at Theale and Blackford near Wedmore built by Richard Carver of Taunton in 1823, or East Horrington and Coxley near Wells in 1838 and 1839. At Blackford, Carver essayed an original octagonal design. The bigger buildings, of which the neighbourhood of Bath and Radstock afford examples, were done in a very free rendering of Perpendicular, in which the nave roof rests on very tall, gawky columns. Such are the naves of Timsbury[2] by G. A. Underwood (1826), Midsomer Norton by Pinch which cost its subscribers £2,829 (1830), Weston near Bath (1830), and Batheaston (1834). More

---

[1] I am indebted for most of these to the Rev. B. F. L. Clarke, author of *Church Builders of the Nineteenth Century*, 1938, whose help and erudition have been most kindly placed at my disposal.

[2] At Timsbury the chancel was extended and transepts added in 1851. The plans of this work, preserved in the Registry at Wells, provide an excellent illustration of the change in Anglican architecture after the Oxford Movement. The 1826 church still had box pews and high pulpit within a few feet of the altar: the plan was of the basilica type with shallow apse. For this subject see Addleshaw and Etchells, *The Architectural Setting of Anglican Worship* (1948), cited above.

interesting are Christ Church, Frome (1817), Combe Down by H. E. Goodridge (1834), and Sampford Brett (1835). Alone among all these Christ Church, Frome, paid some tribute to the local style: at a distant and momentary view its rich traceried windows and parapets give the illusion of the fifteenth century; it was known as the Free Church because there were no pew rents. Its inauguration was attended by much local enthusiasm and a splendid procession, and the author can be proud that his great-grandfather played the principal part in its erection, if he may believe the tribute inscribed on two gilt goblets. Combe Down has a western spire and a great array of attendant spikes; inside, the removal of its arcades and the raising of new aisles late in the century provides an interesting plan and a nave of the unusual aisleless width of some forty-four feet. At Sampford Brett a medieval church was completely transmogrified in 1835: the piers of the crossing were encased in a cluster of white plaster shafts and capitals: little floriated bands of the same material surrounded the windows, and winged cupid heads supported the fine row of fifteenth-century bosses in the roof; a rich overlay of woodcarving smothered the fifteenth-century benches [87].

(2) There are few churches in Somerset, as in England generally, on which the Victorians have not left their too obvious marks, in seating, in stained glass, or in more serious structural repairs and alterations, especially in the chancels. It must be freely conceded that they saved many a church from the complete decay which the long neglect of the past would inevitably have brought, their masonry and workmanship were not invariably bad, but it will be a sorry day if the successive waves of modern taste condone all their glass, their deal pews, their ruthless destruction, and above all their encaustic tiles. Unfortunately the poverty of the mid-twentieth century can rarely undo their lavish legacy.

A more serious charge against the Victorians is their disregard of the local material and of the local style. They had an unfortunate preference for Bath stone which the railways now made as cheap as the product of the neighbouring quarries: its hard, yellow tones, especially in the repaired windows, constantly break in on the soft colours of the old walls and accentuate the mechanical precision of the new carving. Their taste was all for their beloved 'middle pointed', which they regarded as the purest Gothic. Consequently in a county whose golden age was late Perpendicular they erected buildings in a style which, as we have seen, was almost unknown. At Priston or at Christon they had perforce to renovate in a Norman style, and they did it ruthlessly, but whenever they built from the foundations, they built in Decorated. Thus Gilbert Scott built what his admirers regarded as a little gem at Chantry [88a] near Frome, about 1845, and a Taunton architect called Giles built Kingweston in 1855. This, with its flèche, high-pitched roof, and vast, exquisitely carved corbels might more justly be so described. Equally unsuited to their landscape are Stockland Bristol [88b], here illustrated with local figures from a photograph taken shortly after its completion in 1865, West Quantoxhead built by John Norton in 1856 in Doulting stone with piers of pink Babbacombe marble at the vast expense of Sir A. F. Acland Hood, and, above all, Buckland St. Mary, completed in 1863, designed by Ferry and built of flint with Ham Hill dressings. Nothing could be more incongruous than the sudden appearance of this lavish structure in the wild hills on the border of Devon. The wealthy rector who built it, having spared no expense, rendered it all but invisible within by a quantity of windows in the worst designs and the deepest colours by Messrs. Clayton and Bell. Impressed by a monument which he had seen at Berne, he erected a strange memorial to his wife, and the effigy of Louisa Lance bursts through a riven tomb on the chancel floor.

(3) It is too early as yet to examine adequately the work, mostly of restoration and enlargement, done since the late Victorian era. There is nothing of outstanding merit, and much that is careful and correct; if it sometimes offends, it does so by its dullness and lack of character. For its most notable achievement we should have to leave the Anglican Communion and visit Downside, and the author is not prepared for such adventures. Antiquarian sense and perhaps good taste are more widespread now than ever in the past, and the danger of deliberate destruction is in consequence much less. Further, in an age when the churches are so often empty, it is not to be expected that there will be much new building. It will probably be more wholesome and honest if such as there is be done in other than a medieval style. The glories of our great age cannot be copied, but it is our duty, our hope, and our prayer to preserve them for posterity and to enliven them again by worship.

1. EARLY FONTS. (a) Culbone. (b) Nempnett Thrubwell, with fifteenth-century carvings

2. STOGURSEY. (a) Exterior *c.* 1100. (b) Chancel looking west in 1836

82

3. Stogursey. South choir arcade c. 1180

4. LULLINGTON. Norman doorway *c.* 1100

5. STOKE-UNDER-HAM. Norman church with thirteenth-century tower and transept

6. (a) STOKE-UNDER-HAM. Tympanum *c.* 1125. (b) COMPTON MARTIN. From a drawing by J. Buckler, 1835

7. COMPTON MARTIN. South aisle, *c.* 1150

8. COMPTON BISHOP. Churchyard cross seen from thirteenth-century porch

9. Limington. North transept, *c.* 1315

10. SWAINSWICK. Early tower, and ogee arches pre-1340

11. (a) STOKE ST. GREGORY. Thirteenth-century tower, with Perpendicular reconstruction.
(b) NORTH CURRY. Transept and tower *c.* 1320. Chancel *c.* 1450

12. PITMINSTER. Tower and spire, c. 1300

13. WITHAM FRIARY. Church of the lay brethren *c.* 1180. Font 1459

14. (a) YEOVIL. An intact plan of 1370–1400. (b) BRIDGWATER. Tower, thirteenth century. Spire, 1367. Accretion of chantries and chapels *c.* 1400

15. (a) CONGRESBURY. Fourteenth-century spire and clerestory. (b) YATTON. Lower stage of tower and transept, *c.* 1340. Nave and spire, *c.* 1450

16. WEDMORE. (a) From the south-east. (b) From the south-west, in the evening

17. (a) AXBRIDGE. From the north-east. Tower 1380–1440. (b) CREWKERNE. Tower, *c.* 1450. Nave and west front *c.* 1490

18. (a) St. Cuthbert's, Wells. Tower and general reconstruction *c.* 1420. (b) St. John's, Glastonbury. Tower and general reconstruction *c.* 1470

98

19. ILMINSTER. From the north-east. 1450–1510

20. ST. CUTHBERT'S, WELLS. Re-use of thirteenth-century capitals in fifteenth-century arcade

21. MARTOCK. Nave arcade, *c.* 1500

22. QUEEN CAMEL. Fourteenth-century arcade, fifteenth-century screen and roofs

23. NORTH CADBURY. *c.* 1425. Benches 1538

24. LONG SUTTON. Nave consecrated 1493

25. WESTON ZOYLAND. Fifteenth and sixteenth centuries

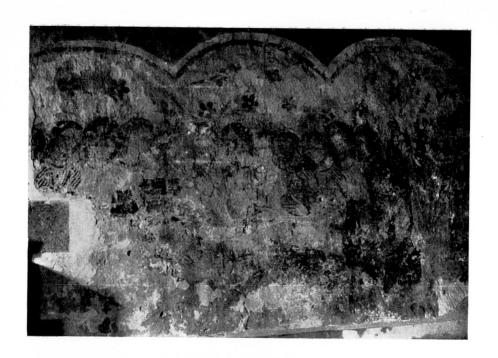

26. (a) Sutton Bingham. Dormition of the Virgin, *c.* 1300. (b) North Cadbury. South door and aisle, *c.* 1425

27. NORTON-SUB-HAMDON. South aisle, c. 1500

28. MARTOCK. South aisle and parapets

29. YATTON. South porch, c. 1450

30. MELLS. South porch, *c.* 1490

31. Curry Rivel. South porch, c. 1505

32. BROOMFIELD. North aisle, 1535

33. ILE ABBOTS. North aisle, *c.* 1535

34. (a) LEIGH-ON-MENDIP. From the south-east, *c.* 1490. (b) KINGSBURY EPISCOPI. From the north-east Tower, *c.* 1510. Eastern sacristy

35. (a) CROWCOMBE. South aisle. (b) BRYMPTON D'EVERCY. Church and house from the west

36. ILE ABBOTS. Base of tower, with statues of the Virgin and Child and the Resurrection

37. WELLS CATHEDRAL. Central tower, *c.* 1320. South-west tower, 1386. North-west tower, 1424

117

38. WRINGTON. Tower, 1420–50

39. EVERCREECH. Tower, *c.* 1450

40. SHEPTON MALLET. Tower, c. 1380. From a Victorian photograph

41. Bishop's Lydeard. Tower, c. 1450

42. NORTON-SUB-HAMDON. Tower, *c.* 1480

43. Backwell. Tower, c. 1470; top reconstructed in seventeenth century

44. BATCOMBE. Tower, 1540

45. CHEWTON MENDIP. Tower, 1541

46. St. Michael's on the Tor, Glastonbury, *c.* 1400

47. Ile Abbots. Tower, *c.* 1480

48. STAPLE FITZPAINE, c. 1485

49. KINGSTON ST. MARY. Tower, *c.* 1490

50. Huish Episcopi. Tower, c. 1505

51. St. Mary Magdalene's, Taunton. 1488–1514

131

52. NORTH PETHERTON. Tower top, from a photograph before 1909

53. NORTH PETHERTON. Tower, *c.* 1515

133

54. (a) HINTON ST. GEORGE. Fifteenth-century couple roof. (b) HALSE. Single-framed wagon roof

55. High Ham. Roofs and screen, 1476

56. St. Decuman's, Watchet. South aisle roof, *c.* 1450. Angels with emblems of the Passion

57. SELWORTHY. South aisle roof, c. 1530

58. MARTOCK. Tie-beam, king post, and panelled roof, 1513

59. SOMERTON. Tie-beam and panelled roof, c. 1520

139

60. SHEPTON MALLET. Panelled wagon roof, c. 1500

61. EAST PENNARD. Nave roof, looking east, *c.* 1490 (*cf.* Plate 24)

62. SOUTH BRENT (Brent Knoll). North aisle roof, *c.* 1510

63. (a) DUNSTER. Screen, 1499. (b) BANWELL. Screen, 1521

143

64. (a) NORTHOVER, near Ilchester, from a drawing in 1847. (b) MOORLINCH,
above Sedgemoor

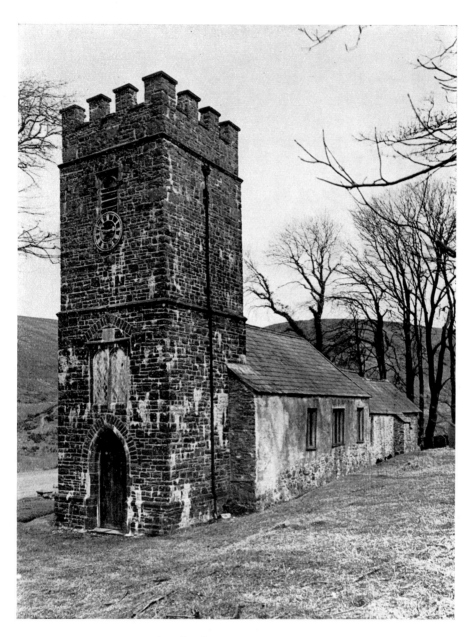

65. OARE, on Exmoor

66. PENDOMER. Sir John de Domer, 1325

67. SOUTH PETHERTON. Sir Giles Daubeney, *c.* 1430

147

68. (a) YATTON. Tombs of Sir Richard Newton *c.* 1470, and of his son, Sir John Newton (right) *c.* 1485. (b) LONG ASHTON. Sir Richard Choke, *c.* 1475

69. HINTON ST. GEORGE. Sir Hugh Poulett, *c.* 1560

149

70. (a) Low Ham. From the north-east, seventeenth-century Gothic. (b) Selworthy. From the south-east. South aisle *c.* 1530

71. Low Ham. Interior. Screen of the Restoration

72. ASHINGTON. Thirteenth, fifteenth, seventeenth and nineteenth centuries

73. MUCHELNEY. Roof *c.* 1625

74. (a) WYKE CHAMPFLOWER. 1624. (b) AXBRIDGE. Roof, 1636. Fifteenth-century nave

75. EAST BRENT. Benches *c.* 1480. Roof, 1637. Gallery, 1635; moved west, 1824

76. CROSCOMBE. Screen and pulpit, 1616. Chancel roof, 1664

77. STOCKLINCH. The lower church of St. Mary Magdalene

78. CURRY RIVEL. Robert and Marmaduke Jennings, 1630

158

79. GOATHURST. Nicholas Halswell, 1633

80. RODNEY STOKE. Sir Edward and Lady Rodney, 1657

81. HINTON ST. GEORGE. John Lord Poulett, *c.* 1665

82. BRUTON. William Godolphin, 1636

83. St. Decuman's, Watchet. Sir John Wyndham, 1634

84. BABINGTON. 1750

85. CAMELEY. Eighteenth-century interior

86. PAULTON. Tower, 1757

87. SAMPFORD BRETT. Chancel, 1835

167

88. (a) CHANTRY. Sir Gilbert Scott c. 1845. (b) STOCKLAND BRISTOL. 1865

ILLUSTRATIONS

[1] All the negatives of the drawings by J. and J. C. Buckler were made by H. St. George Gray.

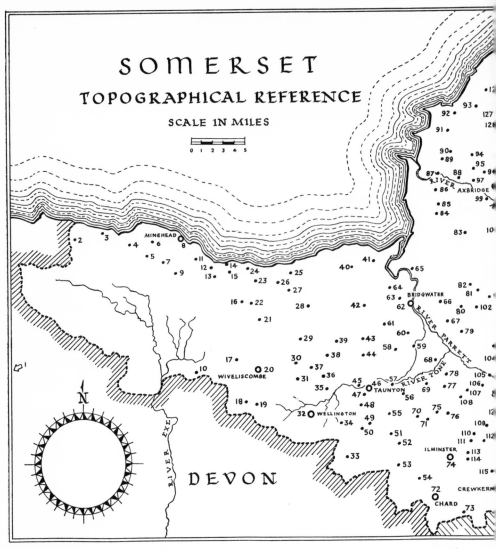

SOMERSET
TOPOGRAPHICAL REFERENCE
SCALE IN MILES

DEVON

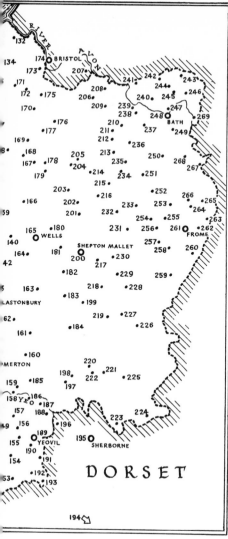

INDEX

Stocklinch, small church, 57
Stogursey, Norman church, 18–19
Stoke St. Gregory, pulpit, 70; tower, 21, 22
Stoke-under-Ham, Norman church, 19
Stone, Nicholas, 72, 73
Sutton Bingham, Norman work, 18; wall painting, 36
Sutton Mallet, eighteenth-century type, 76
Swainswick, tower, 41
Swell, small church, 57

Taunton St. James, font, 56; tower, 44, 45; St. Mary, arcade, 35; date, 33; font, 56; masons, 44; monument, 74; tower, 33, 45, 47, 48
Theale, nineteenth-century church, 77
Thorne, small church, 57
Thornfalcon, bench-ends, 56; sculpture, 58
Thurlbear, Norman work, 18
Thurloxton, pulpit, 70
Tickenham, tower, 44
Timberscombe, screen, 54, 55
Timsbury, nineteenth-century plans, 77
Tintinhull, chancel, 21; churchwardens' accounts, 22 f.
Towers, central, 22, 31, 44; characteristic type, 39; height, 43, 45, 46, 48; octagonal, 23; Quantock, 43, 44–8
Tracery, Gloucestershire type, 46; Midland and Somerset compared, 46; west Somerset type, 38
Trent, spire, 28 f.
Trull, bench-ends, 34, 56; glass, 60; pulpit, 56; screen, 54

Ubley, spire, 28 f.
Underwood, G. A., 77

Vivian-Neal, A. W., 12, 17 f., 19 f., 55 f.

Wadham, monuments at Ilminster, 29, 65
Wall paintings, 36
Walter, H. B., 15
Warman, Simon, 34
Watchet, St. Decuman's, roof, 51; sculpture, 58; Wyndham monuments, 65, 72, 74
Weare, tower, 42
Weaver, F. W., 33 f., 34 f., 36 f.
Webb, Geoffrey, 72
Wedmore, brasses, 73; description, 30; lectern, 56; plan, 29, 30; roof, 52; tower, 30, 42; tracery, 37
Wellington, monument, 74; woodwork, 39

Wellow, date, 33; porch, 37; roof, 52; screen, 55
Wells, Cathedral, 23, 61; chain-gate, 28; school of sculptors, 61, 62, 63; towers, 40, 41–2
Wells, St. Cuthbert's, monument, 73; piers, 23, 35; pulpit, 69; roof, 49, 52; tower, 31, 41; tracery, 37
Wembdon, quarries, 26
West Buckland, arcade, 21; tower, 33
West Coker, monument, 74
West Cranmore, tower, 43
West Harptree, spire, 28 f.
West Pennard, screen, 55
West Quantoxhead, nineteenth-century church, 79
Weston (near Bath), nineteenth-century church, 77; tower, 44
Weston Bampfylde, tower, 23 f.
Weston Zoyland, and Glastonbury, 23; roof, 52; screen, 36, 53; Somerset pier, 36; tower, 43, 45; transept, 33
Whatley, spire, 28 f.
Wheatley, W. W., 58
White Lackington, monument, 73
Wick St. Lawrence, pulpit, 56
Williton, font, 74 f.
Wills, evidence of, 33, 47, 66
Wilton, Saxon work, 17
Winford, tower, 44
Winscombe, glass, 60; tower, 42
Winsham, rood, 55
Witham Friary, relics of, 23
Withycombe, screen, 54
Wiveliscombe, monument, 74
Wolsey, Cardinal, 21
Wolverston, spire, 28 f.
Woodforde, Dr. C., 59, 60
Wookey, tower, 44
Woolley, eighteenth-century church, 75
Wootton Courtney, roof, 51
Worle, pulpit, 56; spire, 28 f.
Wraxall, monument, 64
Wrington, roof, 52; tower, 41
Wyke Champflower, seventeenth-century church, 67, 68
Wynford, William, 26

Yatton, churchwardens' accounts, 28, 29; description, 28; Newton monuments, 28, 63–4; porch, 28, 37; screen, 54; spire, 28, 29; timber on wall surfaces, 28; tower, 28; tracery, 37; west front, 28
Yeovil, description, 25–6; lectern, 56; tracery, 26, 37